The Rock Crusher

A Model for Flow-Based Backlog Management

By Steve Adolph, Shane Hastie, and Ryland Leyton

Published by International Institute of Business Analysis, Toronto, Ontario, Canada.

Print Edition ISBN: 978-1-927584-34-7

eBook Edition ISBN: 978-1-927584-35-4

Any inquiries regarding this publication, requests for usage rights for the material herein, or corrections should be emailed to info@iiba.org.

Dedication

Steve: To my greatest teacher, my daughter, Sophia.

Shane: To my wife, Nancy-your support and encouragement enable me to thrive.

Ryland: To my husband, Mike, for his support and understanding in this project and in my life.

In Memoriam

The hardest single part of building a software system is deciding precisely what to build. No other part of the conceptual work is so difficult as establishing the detailed technical requirements. ... No other part of the work so cripples the resulting system if done wrong. No other part is more difficult to rectify later.

~ Frederick P. Brooks Jr., *No Silver Bullet*

Dr. Brooks passed away while we were writing this book.[1] He was truly a pioneer of the computing profession and an inspiration for generations of software engineers. Among many other achievements, he was the first person to coin the term "computer architecture" and was the father of the 8-bit byte. The world and our industry are worse off for his passing.

1. Hastie, S. *Mythical Man Month Author and Father of the 8-Bit Byte, Fred Brooks, Dies at 91.* InfoQ, December 6, 2022. https://www.infoq.com/news/2022/12/fred-brooks-obituary/.

Preface

For many of us, the Agile Manifesto was a breath of fresh air, an affirmation of what we thought was the right way to create and deliver software.

Why? Because it described a collaborative approach to coping with the hardest part of building a software system: choosing what to build.

The late Fred Brooks, one of the grand elders of software engineering, said in the early 1980s that the hardest part of building a software system is "deciding precisely what to build." That sentiment echoed in the third value of the Agile Manifesto, which calls for "customer collaboration over contract negotiation." The agile principles go on to emphasize that businesspeople and developers must work together daily to harness change for the customers' competitive advantage.

The heart of most Agile methodologies is the backlog, a beautiful and elegant approach to coping with changing requirements. Owned by a product owner, the backlog was supposed to be the single source of work for a team. There would be no ambiguity about what to do next, because all work came from the backlog. Determining precisely what to build would be a conversation between individuals rather than throwing documents over a wall. The coordination delays, the ambiguities, the scrambling to meet arbitrary process-oriented milestones would disappear, replaced by continuous objective feedback and learning that created superior economic value.

As agile coaches and consultants, we get called into organizations that are seeking improvement, which means we don't hear from the teams that were able to realize the agile ideal. This may skew our data, but in our experience many teams, maybe even most teams, have not been able to realize the benefits of agile software development and business agility. One root cause, in our assessment, is a model of backlog management that does not address the needs of teams and enterprises that operate outside that agile ideal.

To cope with the organizational reality facing most teams, we need to rethink the backlog. The core of our argument is simple: the backlog is a key tool for enabling the agile enterprise, yet guidance on how to manage it in any real enterprise context is woefully inadequate. Many agile methodologists do not want to be seen as prescriptive, but people need more than two or three paragraphs on how to manage such a critical component of driving great economic outcomes.

We believe this shortage of guidance has resulted in the challenges we have seen at most of our clients: a backlog that is merely a reservoir of precommitted work, and teams that are at best doing incremental development-some not even that, given the way that they carry over backlog items from iteration to iteration.

However, many clients do get it. We have seen clients who benefit from real customer collaboration, who can quickly test value hypotheses and learn what is really valuable, who have developed good practices for managing their backlog in the real world.

This book captures the practices we have seen in these successful agile teams-the teams that get it and enable their whole organization to benefit from the promises underlying agility and agile approaches.

Going Beyond Software Engineering

All three of us have extensive software engineering experience and so may have a software engineering bias, but the artifacts, roles, and practices we present here go well beyond software engineering and Agile software development methodologies. Agility is not just for software engineering: It is a well-known strategy for economic success. It could even be argued that the software community appropriated the term agility.

The concept of value streams becomes important to support our agility at this stage. As Rather and Shook observed, "wherever there is a product there is a value stream."[1] This is true whether we are writing software, maintaining infrastructure, designing cyber-physical systems, or just organizing volunteers for a community event. We can classify activities in the value stream as either determining precisely what to do or doing it. Agility in any context explicitly incorporates a fast learning cycle: Hypothesize what we should do, do it, learn, repeat. From what we have observed, most organizations have broken value streams, with the "determining precisely what to do" steps hidden or disconnected from the "doing it" part. This impedes or altogether blocks the most valuable aspect of agility: learning what we should really be building.

1. Rother, M., and Shook, J. *Learning to See: Value-Stream Mapping to Create Value and Eliminate Muda, 20th anniversary edition*. Version 1.5. Lean Enterprise Institute. 2018.

How Did The Rock Crusher Come to Be?

The Rock Crusher has been nearly a decade in the making since its humble beginnings in a New Jersey bar. Here is each author's version of the story.

Steve Adoph

Like how much of software engineering and agile development has emerged, the initial concept for The Rock Crusher emerged on the back of a beer mat. In the winter of 2012, I was working with a very cool marquis instrumentation client in New Jersey. The client had taken us to their favorite bar, and we began discussing agile concepts, and particularly how the backlog worked. I found myself sketching the backlog - yes on the back of a beer mat. At this point our client said "oh, I get it, I use to work in materials handling and it's kind of like a Rock Crusher, you guys should change the way you draw this, it would be so much easier to understand." He then proceeded to sketch a caricature of what we today are calling the Rock Crusher. I wish I had kept that beer mat, it would have been cool to have had a shot of it in this book.

But after that, so much of the metaphor made sense to me and it really threw into sharp relief the problems I had observed with the way many organizations have implemented their backlogs. The traditional model of backlog management or what we are calling the stacked plates model simply begs to be a reservoir and disconnects the team from the organization. A reservoir breaks the value stream. There is no concept of flow, and no explicit means for removing less valuable contents. There is no concept of turbulence and managing that turbulence for economic gain. The process of how things actually got into that backlog is hidden behind an overworked or disinterested product owner.

After this I started sketching backlogs using The Rock Crusher model to explain the backlog to my clients. The key learning was turning the backlog upside down to highlight how work items flowed through the backlog. The funnel shape of the backlog immediately implied far more work enters the backlog than could drain out through the bottom which implied the existence of a waste gate.

What really kept me thinking about The Rock Crusher was a number of clients that I worked with who referred to their backlog management process as "rock crushing" or described patterns of backlog management that aligned with The Rock Crusher metaphor. The Rock Crusher was not a new idea, rather it is a model for capturing common success stories.

Long before The Rock Crusher, Shane Hastie had been a professional colleague who was introduced to me by mentor Philippe Kruchten. Shane is not only my colleague, but I regard him as my personal friend. He invited me to join a group of thought leaders collaborating with IIBA to create a set of guidelines for applying the agile mindset to agile business analysis. This was the *Agile Extension to the BABOK Guide®* version 2.

This is where I met Ryland. My personal perspective on Ryland is that between the 3 of us, he is the most grounded. While Shane and I advocate and work with clients to improve their ways of working, Ryland makes his bread and butter doing real work as a practicing business analyst. One running joke we have is that I generally write like an academic (I do have a PhD and after that indoctrination it is really hard to write human). Ryland is wonderful in saying "Steve, ...no." and translating my academic arrogance into something that is approachable by people who are just trying to get a job done.

After completing the *Agile Extension to the BABOK Guide®* version 2., the three of us began informally collaborating on The Rock Crusher concept, often incorporating the ideas into our teaching and consulting. For example Shane published #noprojects with Evan Leybourne which included an early representation of The Rock Crusher.

Things really took off when IIBA invited me to contribute to IIBA's Knowledge Hub. This sort of strapped on the boosters and inspired us to keep on going and write the book. The pandemic hit at the same time and there is only so much Netflix binging you can do while social isolating. So two years later, after a lot of work, revisions, more revisions, and even more revisions I hope we have captured all those ideas and patterns in a manner you find helpful.

Shane Hastie

As Steve mentions, we were introduced by Philippe Kruchten sometime around 2008. Philippe was a fairly frequent visitor to SoftEd in New Zealand, speaking at our conferences and presenting his master classes. One of his ideas that strongly resonated with me was explicitly calling out different types of work in the product backlog.[1] He also mentioned this Canadian chap Steve who was doing some interesting things with backlogs and product agility. We invited Steve to the SDC conference in Wellington and Sydney in 2010 and this became the foundation for a firm friendship and lots of collaboration over the years.

At that time, there was a bit of a schism between the agile development community and the business analysis community. In 2008 I listened to a talk where the role of the analyst in agile development was described as being "the copy boy" for the development team. This inspired me to write an article sharing my perspective on the value of having an analyst on the team.[2] This was my first experience with publishing something, and led to me taking on a part-time role as news editor for InfoQ.com.

---

1. Hastie, S. *What Color Is Your Backlog?* InfoQ. May 2, 2010. www.infoq.com/news/2010/05/what-color-backlog/.

At that stage I was heavily involved as a volunteer with IIBA in New Zealand and Australia. I got involved with the initial work writing the first version of the *Agile Extension to the BABOK® Guide* and advocated for it to become a joint effort of the Agile Alliance and IIBA. Version 1 was a reasonable starting point, but we knew that the ideas would evolve as they were applied in the wild, and lots of new learning would emerge.

When it was time for version 2, Steve was one of the thought leaders who stepped up to share his ideas. Ryland joined the team, along with James King, Kent McDonald, Stephanie Vineyard, Jas Phul, and Paul Stapleton. The discussions were enlightening, and it was a wonderful collaboration activity. Friendships were forged and deepened, and we were keen to find ways to continue the collaboration.

Steve and I had been talking about writing a book for years and had thrown lots of ideas into a virtual pot to see what came out as the thinking simmered. Steve was definitely the driver, taking the often unformed thoughts and giving them structure and academic rigor. As we continued putting them together, we realized that we needed the perspective of an active practitioner to turn our somewhat abstract ideas into practical advice. Both of us had been impressed by and enjoyed working with Ryland on the Agile Extension, so it was logical to invite him along on the ride. Fortunately, he was keen to be involved and joined us on the rollercoaster.

A note on crushing rocks: Early in my career as a systems analyst working on data processing products (sometime in the late 1980s) I worked on automating processes for mining companies. One of my strongest memories is of visiting a diamond mine in the Kimberlite fields in South Africa. There they blast large chunks of rock out of ancient volcanic pipes and put the rocks through a series of crushers, discarding the waste and filtering out the gems-in this case, real diamonds. It was fascinating to see how much work goes into extracting the gems and how much waste it creates. Even then I could see the analogy to identifying the real requirements for the products we were building-there were so many good ideas that weren't worth implementing when we examined them. When Steve first mentioned the rock crusher metaphor, it immediately reminded me of visiting the mine and of how this lines up with my experience over multiple decades.

If you take nothing else away from this book, do please implement a waste gate on your backlog and use it to filter out the real gems that constitute customer and business value.

2. Hastie, S. *The Role of the Analyst in Agile Projects*. InfoQ. December 5, 2008. www.infoq.com/articles/agile-business-analyst-role/.

Ryland Layton

I had the pleasure of meeting Steve and Shane during work on IIBA's *Agile Extension to the BABOK® Guide* version 2. At that point in my career, I was surprised to be in the room with them and the rest of the team!

To summarize working with Steve and Shane in just a sentence or two, Steve was a towering academic who usually could cite several sources relevant to the point he was making. Shane, meanwhile, was a cross between Santa, because of his beard, and Yoda, because of his deep knowledge and insights which are often framed as a question.

As for myself, I agree I tend to take the practitioner view of things: How will the average "analyst in the street" use this? Is this information accessible? Can it be applied easily in their work?

Between that view, and the heavy thinking often expressed during *Agile Extension* working sessions, I had a funny moment relating to a particular contribution to our work together. People could take a long time, sometimes three to five minutes, explaining that they loved a particular thought and idea. These ideas were in fact just great-truly valuable!-but perhaps a little far afield from the topics for the *Agile Extension*. After this happened several times, I proposed that we replace those conversations with the phrase "that sounds like a great topic for your next book." This would stand in for the lengthy (and respectful) conversation, and we could still talk about the subject if we needed to.

We all found ourselves on the listening end of that phrase.

In short, it became a good working relationship, and when we were done with the *Agile Extension* I certainly missed their company.

In 2021, Steve and Shane included me in their early review group to look at the rough manuscript of the book you are now reading. I liked it. I really liked it, and I feel the ideas presented are very valuable to the analyst toolkit and to those who are seeking better practice and want to create positive organizational change.

A few days after I read it, I walked around my backyard on my phone while Steve and I threw ideas back and forth about the book, the directions it could go, and what it needed to get there. I mentioned I thought the writing was excellent but, as he notes, needed some grounding in the core of the matter for the reader, and to stay away from distracting topics. I offered to help with this if they were considering another author. Steve immediately told me he and Shane had been trying to figure out how to ask me so, yes, they were up for it.

I'm happy to have made contributions to the book and added some ideas, and I think I did add clarity and brevity in parts. However, I must emphasize that the work came from Steve and Shane. I am very happy to have been included in what they started and shaped.

That said, if you read this whole book and still feel something is missing, such as another 200 pages on this topic, contact Steve or check out the website at RockCrusher.org.

Finally, a word on what I find so appealing about this book. I love how the Rock Crusher helps show the actual work that is done in product design and ideation. So much of this is hidden in actual practice that it becomes frustrating for analysts, product professionals, and developers. We hear things like "You just have to get the requirements! How hard is it !?!?" from people who are new to the field, or who don't understand that-as Steve points out-deciding what to build is really, really, really important. It is also no small effort to make those choices.

I also was a fan of the Rock Crusher manuscript for showing how to set this system up, explaining how to make the work and the flow visible in an organization, and describing the value this would bring. So many people try to create real change and have a hard time showing the way, creating a vision, and walking the path. I think this book can help by giving you a good, solid approach to such change.

I hope you will find this as interesting and valuable as I do. My best wishes to you as you apply the principles and techniques in your workplace.

Acknowledgments and Appreciations

We are not the first to say that "It Takes A Village", and we'd like to appreciate the following people and organizations for their help.

First, the International Institute of Business Analysis. We are very proud to be the first formal book from IIBA Publications. We did not choose this lightly - there were other options, we preferred them. We chose IIBA because we felt that the mission, vision, and values of the organization were strongly aligned with our own, and that this would result in greatest service to the analyst and product communities.

Second, the work of IIBA team members Paul Stapleton, Tiffani Iacolino, Yana Kelly, and Scott Lidstone, in the creation of the book itself. The success of the end product would simply not have been possible without your strong, mindful, and collaborative work.

We wish to thank our professional editor, DeAnna Burghart, not only for being a pleasure to work with but also for her professional skill, her knowledge of the domains of business analysis and agility, and her patience in working with the three of us. DeAnna truly is a master of the art of cat herding.

Being a professional reviewer of a book is a commitment of time and thinking. We'd like to appreciate our reviewers for their contribution: Kevin Brennan, Barb Carkenord, Rita Emmons, James King, John Kosco, Evan Leybourn, Kent McDonald, Johanna Rothman, and Craig Smith. You are all strong members of the field and your opinions and feedback have been valuable to each of us as authors and professionals. You have our sincerest thanks for your help.

Endorsements

"*Agile approaches are now accepted practice and while the fundamentals of the agile mindset remain the same, we have seen a constant evolution in how we write code, create stories, and scale our collaboration. In that time, while so many things have evolved, the humble backlog has continued to sit in the background, useful, but barely different from its original conception. This book provides an overdue evolution of the backlog, embracing its strengths and confronting its challenges to reimagine what how it can be used in the modern agile organization. If the Rock Crusher is a reimagined backlog though, it is alsomore than that.*

The Rock Crusher becomes a holistic set of approaches that enable the team to improve flow and value across the organization."

— James King, Agile Coach

"*Finally someone has splashed a dose of reality onto the broken flat backlog metaphor! Lots of great concepts and tools here.*"

— Jeff Patton, Chief Troublemaker
www.jpattonassociates.com

Table of Contents

1. Introducing The Rock Crusher

Learning Objectives

After reading this chapter, you should be able to explain:
- the value and benefit of the backlog,
- the economic consequences of a broken value stream,
- how our current model of backlog management can break the value stream by impeding flow and disconnecting the team, and
- at a high level, the benefits of the Rock Crusher model for backlog management.

The backlog is a beautiful, powerful, and delightfully simple tool for managing work in modern agile organizations. It is the single repository from which a team pulls its next most valuable work item. The backlog fosters agility by enabling the additions, removal, reprioritization, and, most importantly, visualization of all the potential work for a product.

The product owner facilitates this simplicity by representing a single clear line of content authority. According to the Scrum Guide, the product owner is "accountable for effective Product Backlog management."[1] Simply put, the product owner is accountable for ensuring that the development team works on the right things. This arrangement helps businesses avoid the horrendous waste that's created when developers are forced to spend time and effort coordinating competing work requests rather than doing the work.

---

1. Schwaber, K., and Sutherland, J. *The Scrum Guide*. 2020.

This change in how we conceptualized and authorized work-combined with values and principles expressed in the Agile Manifesto-was a true paradigm shift in how teams got the job done.

Since the Agile Manifesto was published in February 2001, agile has matured from an umbrella term for a collection of lightweight, team-based software methodologies to a strategy for business success. Agile development, Lean, and Systems Thinking were integrated to address the challenges of the digital enterprise. Agile grew from just "uncovering better ways of developing software" (agilemanifesto.org) to uncovering better ways to create the agile enterprise.

Stacked Plates and Broken Value Streams

The most common visual representation of a backlog is one that looks like a stack of plates where each backlog item appears to be the same as any other. Backlog items are stacked and processed in sequence. This model implies that the backlog is prioritized with forced ranking and that all the items are at a similar level of abstraction and readiness, which is rarely the case.

Figure 1.1: The stacked plates metaphor for the backlog

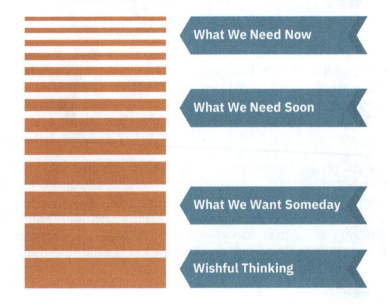

What We Need Now

What We Need Soon

What We Want Someday

Wishful Thinking

Lean thinking is integral to Agile, and the holy grail of Lean is *flow*. Flow makes knowledge and materials available when needed at each step in the value stream.[1] We can use value streams to help us understand how the stacked plates model breaks the value stream and impedes flow.

A value stream is simply a model of how we deliver a product or service, from a trigger event to the delivery of value to a customer. What is sometimes called "concept to cash." Value streams are a simple yet potent tool for understanding how we get things done. As Rother and Shook observed, "wherever there is a product for the customer, there is a value stream."[2]

Figure 1.2: A value stream

Most team-based agile methodologies assume that the value stream begins and ends with the product owner, who owns the backlog and accepts the continuous flow of increments from the team. This model fits well within the Lean concept of flow, where the product owner makes materials available in small bite-sized chunks as the team needs them and accepts them as the team delivers them.

1. Ward, A., and Sobek, D. *Lean Product and Process Development, 2nd ed.* Lean Enterprise Institute. 2014.

2. Rother, M., and Shook, J. *Learning to See, 20th anniversary ed.* Lean Enterprise Institute. 2018.

Figure 1.3: Most agile methodologies assume the value stream begins and ends with the product owner

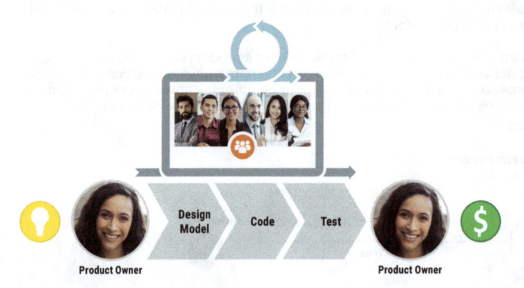

However, this is rarely the situation. More likely, the value stream extends much further, with steps both upstream and downstream of the product owner. The agile team, hidden behind the product owner, is blissfully unaware of those upstream and downstream steps.

Figure 1.4: Upstream and downstream steps hidden behind the product owner

Fuller and Kruchten explain how this disconnection leads to low product quality. In their study, teams with short horizons of interest

> *"were less likely to take collective responsibility for the product's current success or failure. With a (near-term) narrow lens on the product plan, they would take ownership for the work they performed, but not the overall product result. They are more likely to passively criticise than attempt to understand the vision and broader plan-"It isn't the strategy I would have put together" or "I don't think they understand the market very well". The strong 'they' language indicated lack of ownership and/or strongly held opinions coupled with a sense of having little control or influence."[1]*

Organizations often unintentionally break their value stream by adopting hybrid waterfall-agile methodologies, derisively referred to as agi-fall or waterscrumming. The backlog becomes a committed reservoir of work that buffers the different flow rates between the agile team and the organization. While the agile team can blissfully pretend to be delivering a flow of value, all this does is erect walls around the development team.

---

1. Fuller, R., and Kruchten, P. *Blurring Boundaries: Toward the Collective Empathic Understanding of Product Requirements.* Information and Software Technology 140, no. 106670 (December 2021).

Figure 1.5: Hybrid methodologies erect walls around the development team and break flow

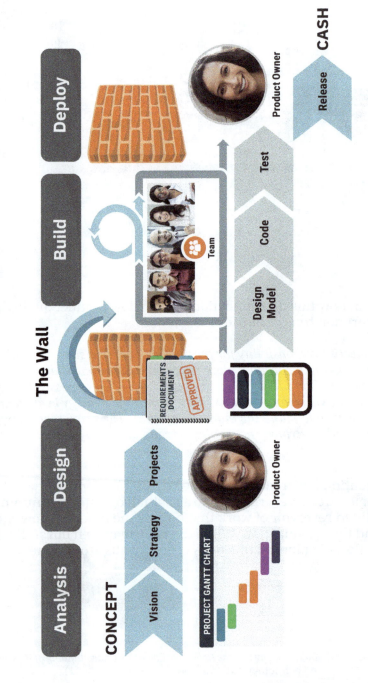

Introducing The Rock Crusher

The economic consequences of a broken value stream are significant, as even the much-vaunted Toyota Motor Corporation learned. In their book *Competing Against Time*[1] (and in Stalk's related article in Harvard Business Review), George Stalk and Thomas Hout tell the story of Toyota's broken value stream and how it squandered their manufacturing gains.

> *Until the 1980s, Toyota was organized as Toyota Motor Manufacturing, which built cars, and Toyota Motor Sales, which sold and distributed cars-technology and business in separate organizations. In the late 1970s, Toyota Motor Manufacturing could build a car in less than two days. However, the entrenched bureaucracy at Toyota Motor Sales took nearly a month to process a sales order and deliver a vehicle. According to Stalk and Hout, "Twenty to 30 percent of the cost of a car to a customer, which was more than it cost Toyota to manufacture the car, and more than 90 percent of the time the customer had to wait was consumed by the sales and distribution function." We can imagine the frustration this created for Taiichi Ohno when the whole point of the Toyota Production System was to reduce the timeline "from the moment the customer gives us an order to the point when we collect the cash."[2]*

In 1982, the frustration boiled over and the two companies were merged. The executives and directors of Toyota Motor Sales were replaced by executives and directors trained in Lean thinking. New processes and new management information systems supporting those processes were developed. By 1987, the sales cycle from order to delivery was reduced from a month to just six days.

This time compression was far more than a cost-saving exercise. Toyota gained a massive competitive advantage because they were able to go from "selling whatever was on the lot" to "selling what the customer wanted." The short cycle times meant Toyota could exploit fast learning cycles and discover what cars customers wanted. By reducing their timelines and embracing change, they were able to turn over units more quickly and command higher margins on their sales.

Toyota's experience teaches us that manufacturing excellence is not enough. Even if our developers are excellent agile coders, a broken value stream will destroy product agility. Ask yourself what processes are upstream of the product owner and how agile they are. How fast is the product feedback loop? How quickly can you learn what your customers really want and incorporate that learning into your product? How quickly can you gain economic advantage from that learning?

1. Stalk, G. *Time-The Next Source of Competitive Advantage*. Harvard Business Review, July 1988. https://hbr.org/1988/07/time-the-next-source-of-competitive-advantage.

2. Stalk, G., and Hout, T. *Competing Against Time: How Time-Based Competition Is Reshaping Global Markets*. Simon and Schuster. 1990.

As the agile mindset has grown in the larger business community, we have found that the stacked plates backlog model and hybrid methodologies create significant impediments to creating value:

- *Impeded Flow.* Flow is critical to value creation in the agile business because sustainably and continuously delivering value accelerates learning. Without flow, there is no agility. Unfortunately, the backlog often breaks the value stream and serves as a requirements reservoir rather than a beautiful tool for rapidly evolving a product.

- *Loss of Customer Focus.* The stacked plates model encourages a project-based approach to software development by disconnecting the team from the customer. The team focuses on technical delivery rather than satisfying the customer.

- *Overprocessing.* A disconnected, coding-centric development team often requires overly detailed technical specifications. This can result in backlog items that are really just detailed, predigested specifications that the development team takes as rote instructions rather than a conversation starter. When this happens we lose a key agile advantage: customer collaboration.

- *False Precision and Needless Sequencing.* The stack of plates model tends to encourage the perception that the backlog consists of many small, fine-grained backlog items ordered by forced ranking. This perception can introduce unnecessary sequencing based on technical dependency-which should be handled by skilled team members during design, not by reducing the backlog items well below the point of value to the end customer.

- *Unrealistic Product Owner Role.* The product owner role puts unrealistic expectations on the individual holding it for all but the shortest value streams or the smallest teams. Outside these narrow exceptions, the product owner is expected to have a breadth and depth of skills that are technically possible but often practically unlikely, rare, or very expensive in the talent marketplace.

The Product Owner: Only Superhumans Need Apply

The product owner role described in most agile methodologies is unrealistic.[1] Viewing the product owner as the sole owner of the backlog ignores all the roles necessary to manage value. In many situations, code development constitutes less than 40% of the effort to go from idea to delivered software solution. There is a significant gap in a model that makes a single person responsible for as much as 60% of the value delivery effort.[2]

In most agile practices, the product owners have full authority over and responsibility for their products. From the point of view of most early agile methodologies, the world really did begin and end with the product owner. However, larger scale and complexity increasingly dictate that product owners coordinate with a broader stakeholder community that includes other product owners, product managers, architects, leaders, and subject matter experts from multiple domains.

When we refuse to acknowledge this problem, we bury the hidden costs, effort, inefficiency, and loss of value that it causes. Sometimes the product owner is inappropriately blamed for this, when in reality the agile practices do not inherently surface all the work involved in successfully delivering customer value in most enterprises.

Ask agile coaches about the most common issues they observe with their clients. They will likely call out product ownership, and often mention similar challenges:

- The team lacks time and guidance because the product owner is unavailable.

- Competing product owners do not speak with one voice.

- A product owner is unwilling to use their authority and is being bullied by one or more stakeholders or the team.

- A product owner knows less about their product than the team does and fails to hike up the learning hill.

- A product owner sees themselves as a short-timer and is only interested in their pet project at the expense of the overall product mission, vision, or strategy.

---

1. Stalk and Hout. *Competing Against Time*. Free Press. 2003.
   Martin, A., Biddle, R., and Noble, J. *The XP customer role in practice: Three studies.* Paper presented at the Agile Development Conference, 2004.

2. Yang, Y., He, M., Li, M., Wang, Q., and Boehm, *B.W. Phase distribution of software development effort.* International Symposium on Empirical Software Engineering and Measurement. 2008.

Thoughts from Shane

I was asked to help an organization who builds a number of products on top of a common platform. There were 12 designated product owners and I was working with them to "speed up the rate of product delivery". The organization leadership was frustrated because they had these expensive people who were supposed to ensure that products got released to the market rapidly, and yet the rate at which updates and new products were deployed had gone down since they appointed the product owners to take responsibility for delivery.

As part of the coaching I was doing with the product owners I asked about their decision-making authority. It turned out that all product-related decisions had to be approved by a single individual - the Chief Executive Officer.

The CEO was effectively the real product owner, all of the people appointed to the role were simply acting as conduits to get requests in front of the CEO. The nominal product owners all knew exactly where the bottleneck was and what needed to be done to free up the flow, however no-one in the organization could question the CEO.

This is a situation where being the expensive external consultant was very advantageous - I had access to the CEO (he was the one who had called me in). We updated their Kanban boards to show the extra state of "CEO Approval" and pointing out how long items were sitting in that state and quantified the cost of delay on the items in the backlog.

It took a while for the CEO to let go and empower the product owners, initially by putting a cost/value threshold on backlog items that had to go up to him for approval and slowly over time increasing that threshold so over time only the most expensive backlog items needed his authorization, and eventually he was able to let go entirely.

The Rock Crusher: A Grown-Up Model of Backlog Management

The problems we have highlighted are not a dismissal of backlogs. Instead, we are calling out the misuse and abuse that result from stretching a simple model beyond its original scope. Agile grew up, and so should the backlog.

A grown-up model of the backlog would recognize the reality of enterprise software development. It would enable flow and visualize what Fred Brooks called "the hardest part of building a software system." A grown-up model of backlog management would not disconnect the team from the customer and the product. It would be an active part of the flow and not a passive reservoir. So how can we make our backlog model grow up?

First, if flow is important, we must open both ends of the backlog. Nothing flows through a pipe that is only open at one end. Also, we don't think of flow as going uphill, so we turn the backlog upside down such that ideas flow in through the top and refined, ready work flows out through the bottom.

Figure 1.6: Opening up the backlog to create flow

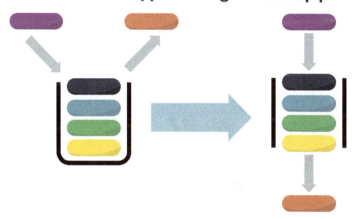

We always have more work than a team can handle, so we need to widen the intake side, or top of the pipe, to handle the flow.

Figure 1.7: Widening the intake to handle the intake flow

We always have more ideas than capacity to deliver

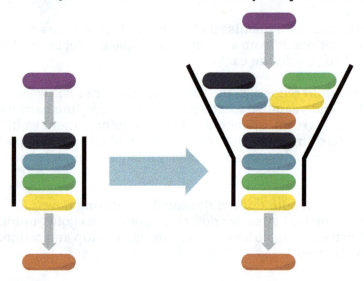

If we have more work than a team can sustainably pull, we need to add a drain or waste gate, to keep the backlog from overflowing.

Figure 1.8: Draining away the excess flow

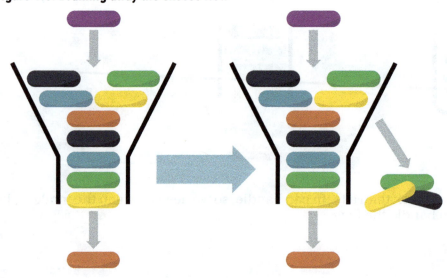

Introducing The Rock Crusher

Finally, we must recognize that the flow is initially turbulent. Ideas arrive at varying times and are of varying size, varying ambiguity, and varying readiness. We need to throttle and stabilize the flow for the team.

Figure 1.9: Throttling and stabilizing a turbulent flow

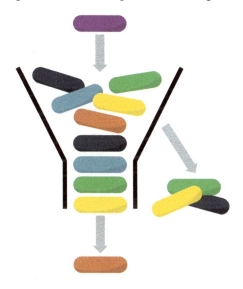

We call this model of backlog management the Rock Crusher. The Rock Crusher replaces the stacked plates metaphor and helps solve the problems it creates. Consider a rock crusher in the real world:

- Large, unrefined items are dropped into the top.
- The items are tumbled and broken into parts.
- Low-value items are discarded.

Figure 1.10: The Rock Crusher

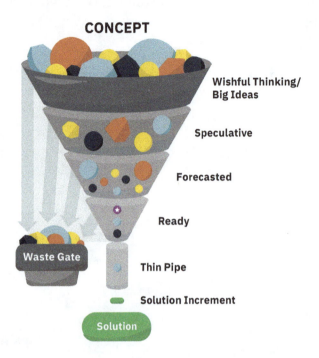

Valuable portions flow deeper into the process; waste products are removed at the same time. Items may tumble for some time, getting refined in the process, but nothing stays in the crusher forever. Eventually, the valuable parts are identified and retained and valueless material is discarded.

Key Rock Crusher Flow Elements

- *Rocks*. The Rock Crusher crushes rock and a rock is just our word for a backlog item-any item of value waiting to be implemented. While many frameworks categorize backlog items by size-for example, stories, and epics-the Rock Crusher does not.

- *The Funnel*. All rocks enter at the top of the Rock Crusher funnel. Rocks may be highly unrefined back-of-the-envelope ideas or reasonably well-refined stories. That is fine-we reject nothing at this stage. As rocks progress through the funnel they are tumbled, elaborated, and refined. The turbulent flow of rocks is throttled and stabilized here. Tumbling rocks are sized, refined, split, reprioritized, and in many cases discarded. The funnel makes this throttling and stabilizing process visible, showing everyone what it takes to determine precisely what to build.

- *The Waste Gate*. As rocks are refined in the funnel, whatever is not valuable exits through the waste gate. As with real-world ore refinement, any given rock may have nothing valuable in it. Nothing is wrong with discarding a whole concept, or most of one. Not every stone holds a diamond, although there is nothing wrong with considering the possibility.

- *The Thin Pipe*. In refinement processes, the thin pipe is a metaphor for the limited capacity of the team. Valuable, well-refined ideas are pulled for construction; other parts of the idea, not yet discarded or accepted, may remain in the tumbling process.

- *The Village*. Not shown in figure 1.10 is the village. This concept acknowledges that one individual cannot manage a backlog on their own. It takes a village of collaborating roles to stabilize and throttle the flow through the backlog.

Rock Crusher Benefits

The Rock Crusher provides several benefits to any business:

- *All the work is made visible*. Authoring code is not the only activity that creates value. Investment in other areas is essential, especially when those investments optimize the value of costly development work.

- *It highlights flow*. When all work is visible, the flow is visible, and we can manage the entire flow-not just the coding steps. Work, value, and circumstances change. We must accommodate this while simultaneously understanding the flow of good product ideation.

- *Not everything gets done*. The stacked plates model implies smooth flow and that putting something in the backlog means it will get done. The Rock Crusher captures the turbulent nature of requirements flow and acknowledges that stabilizing and throttling the flow means discarding many ideas.

- *It takes a village*. Good rock refinement requires the effort of the whole team-or even many teams. It always has. As a decision source for a development team, the product owner is a huge advantage of agile and should never be disregarded. However, the idea that the product owner acts alone up to the moment of that decision is an illusion that hides the value created by the investment in this decision.

Summary

- The backlog is a powerful, compelling, and delightfully simple tool for managing work in modern agile organizations.
- The traditional stack of plates backlog representation breaks the value stream when stretched beyond the team.
- The traditional role description of the product owner does not highlight all the roles required to determine precisely what to build and places an excessive burden on the individual designated as the product owner.
- The Rock Crusher is a flow-based representation of the backlog and helps visualize all the steps and roles required to determine precisely what to build.

Try This

1. Try to identify your value stream for your product by walking the steps in your process between concept and cash.
   a. Is your value stream broken at points (for example, hand-offs with long delays)?
   b. Is your organization hiding flow disruptions and broken value streams behind waterscrumming methodologies that misuse the backlog?
   c. Toyota paid the price for their broken value stream with lost revenue. If your value stream is broken, what price are you paying?
2. How are you throttling work? Does your process assume that work in the backlog will get done eventually, or is there a mechanism for explicitly purging backlog items?
3. Who is the product owner for the backlog?
   a. What do they do?
   b. Do they have help?
   c. Is the product owner you identified a trained product owner, or is someone filling in for the role?

Introducing The Rock Crusher

2   Exploring The Rock Crusher

Learning Objectives

After reading this chapter, you should be able to describe
- the major Rock Crusher components,
- the roles in the village, and
- how the village roles collaborate to refine rocks.

This chapter is an overview of the topics presented in later chapters. We suggest that you read this chapter in full so you can decide which topics are most relevant for you. From there, you can create your own journey, whether that means reading the rest of the book in order or taking a different path.

The Rock Crusher's Components

Figure 2.1: The Rock Crusher

The Rock Crusher is a flow-based model of backlog management for visualizing and managing the work required to create a steady flow of ready work for a team.

Let's unpack that statement.

The Rock Crusher is flow-based because knowledge and work flow toward the solution instead of pooling up in the backlog. The backlog should not be a place where work goes to die.

The Rock Crusher helps with visualizing and managing by ensuring the team can see all the work associated with "deciding precisely what to build,"[1] not just the coding work.

The "steady flow of ready work for the team" is needed because the team is a constrained resource with limited capacity. The team delivers the best value when it has a steady flow of the right work—meaning the team's capacity is not exceeded and

1. Brooks, F. *No Silver Bullet: Essence and Accidents of Software Engineering.* Computer 20, no. 4. 1987.

Exploring The Rock Crusher

the team is not starved for work. Coordination delays and even congestive collapse occur when demand exceeds the team's capacity.

The Rock Crusher is not "yet another methodology." Instead, it integrates common success patterns that many teams use to better visualize and manage their work for getting backlog items—or as we refer to them, rocks—ready. Some organizations even refer to their backlog management processes as "rock crushing." The ideas presented in the Rock Crusher are not inherently new or unique; however, they are not well understood in the wild. This book, based on the distilled experience of the three authors, explains concepts that are frequently overlooked and misused.

There are four crucial conceptual Rock Crusher components for managing the flow of rocks:

- The intake process, which ensures that all work entering the funnel is acknowledged.

- The funnel, which throttles and stabilizes the turbulent flow of rocks.

- The thin pipe through which the team pulls ready rocks.

- The waste gate, which drains excess rocks.

With these four concepts, the Rock Crusher implements a very simple flow equation, what goes in, must come out. All work entering the rock crusher exits either through the thin pipe or is ejected through the waste gate.

The Intake Process

The Rock Crusher has an intake funnel through which all rocks arrive. "All rocks" means everything, from the big long-range roadmapped initiatives to the simple "could you just make this one small change for me" shoulder taps. In general, most new rocks are presented to the team through what we call the front door on a regular cadence at the regular backlog refinement or planning meetings.

Realistically, although it's undesirable, teams also need back door policies in place so they can be responsive to small requests or requests that need to be expedited. The backlog owner is accountable for deciding how urgent, small, or "crisis" requests are handled.

The Funnel

Lean concepts such as flow emerged from manufacturing; as a result, Lean texts often portray flow as a smooth, synchronized, first in, first out flow of work through a production line. Smooth flow may be the norm in manufacturing because there is no discovery process. We know precisely what we are building, and variance is low. However, in product development workflows are necessarily turbulent. As Donald Reinertsen writes, "Value cannot be created without variability."[1]

Software offers so many opportunities for unique products and features that this turbulence is essential in the early ideation phases of development. Kent Beck's mantra, "embrace change," elegantly sums up agile's link between turbulence and value creation.

The Rock Crusher funnel shifts our mental model of the backlog from a passive reservoir to an active learning and discovery process that results in a *stabilized* and *throttled* flow:

- *Stabilized* because the backlog gets prioritized through forced ranking, with few or no changes taking place in the ranking.

- *Throttled* because the flow does not exceed the team's capacity, represented by the thin pipe.

The Rock Crusher's funnel makes sure the progressive stabilization and throttling process is visible and therefore managed by the village, rather than hidden behind the product owner.

1. Reinertsen, D. G. *The principles of product development flow: second generation lean product development,* Celeritas. 2009.

Exploring The Rock Crusher

The Thin Pipe

As previously stated, the thin pipe is a metaphor for the team's limited capacity. Push too many rocks or excessively large rocks through, and the thin pipe will clog and block flow. The team pulls rocks through the thin pipe to deliver a solution increment. How the team creates a solution increment is beyond the scope of the Rock Crusher. The thin pipe simply represents a point at which the team could commit to pulling ready rocks through the subsequent steps in the value stream, such as development or fabrication.

Figure 2.2: The Thin Pipe

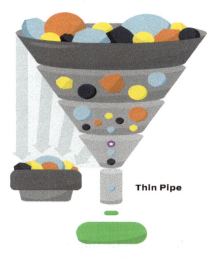

Thin Pipe

The Waste Gate

Figure 2.3: The Rock Crusher waste gate

Only a fraction of what goes into the Rock Crusher's funnel flows out through the thin pipe. To avoid turning the Rock Crusher back into a reservoir of forgotten and zombie rocks, we must discard rocks that are no longer valuable through a waste gate.

The waste gate is a critical Rock Crusher component for implementing a straightforward flow equation: What goes in must come out. The Rock Crusher's funnel is intentionally larger than the thin pipe; after all, just because a rock is in the backlog does not mean it will be done. But leaving obsolete or forgotten rocks in the backlog plugs up the process and flow, creating friction and waste. Good backlog hygiene demands that we constantly remove clutter from the backlog. Unlike the stack of plates visualization, the Rock Crusher explicitly reveals there are two paths out of the backlog: the thin pipe or the waste gate.

Rocks

As obvious as it sounds, the Rock Crusher crushes rocks. A *rock* is the Rock Crusher's metaphor or synonym for a backlog item. A rock can be any work a team may have to do, from a large initiative to a user story to a defect fix. A rock simply represents something we want.

Figure 2.4: All types of work are represented as backlog items, or rocks

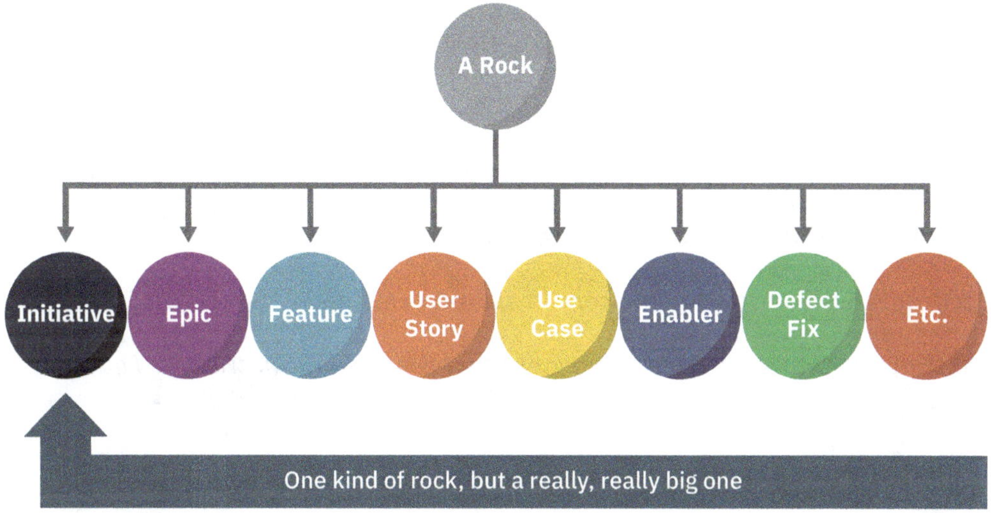

A rock is well formed if it has three attributes:

- An *intent* – It is objectively clear what outcome we want from the rock.

- A *verifiable model* – The intent results in a work product that can be objectively verified as done and that delivers the desired outcome for the rock.

- A *test* – There is an objective, demonstrable way of evaluating whether the verifiable model satisfied the rock's intent.

Figure 2.5: A rock is realized by a verifiable model

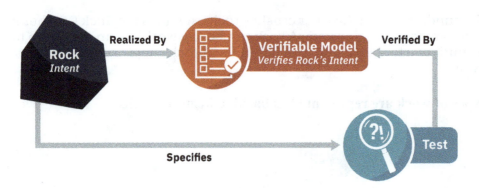

Simply, a well-formed rock is the combination of the statements, "I see what you intended to do and why," "I see what you did do," and "I see the test I can apply to know whether what you did fulfills what you intended to do."

For software teams, a well-written user story is a good example of a well-formed rock:

> *As a frequent flier I want to see my point balance so that I can determine whether I qualify for a free flight.*
>
> *Acceptance Criteria:*
> * *Point balance is viewable on both desktop and mobile devices.*
> * *Point balance is prominently displayed with point goal necessary for free flight.*

The intent of this story should be reasonably clear, and when we combine it with the acceptance criteria we could probably create a good set of tests to verify that the resulting software satisfies the intent. Compare this story to the following poorly written story:

> *Frequent flier point balance lookup.*

This story is at best ambiguous, and it would be hard to objectively know when it is done.

Much of what the Rock Crusher is about is managing the turbulent process for refining poorly formed rocks into well-formed ready rocks that the team can pull through the thin pipe.

Solutions and Solution Increments

When the team pulls ready rocks through the thin pipe, they create and test the rock's verifiable model. If the verifiable model is accepted by the backlog owner, the rock becomes a *solution increment* that contributes to a solution. A *solution* is a product or service that creates value for the enterprise. It could be a long-term revenue-generating product or a temporary endeavor such as a project.

In the Rock Crusher model, teams are organized around solutions. Rocks represent work that increases (or at least defends) the value of the solution. The value of any given rock is expressed in terms of the value it adds to the solution.

The Village—Rock Crusher Roles

Figure 2.6: It takes a village. One person cannot do it all.

Classic backlog management is usually described as a collaboration between an omniscient, omnipotent product owner and a team. This model does not work for most organizations because the product owner role is so demanding that it's too much for one person to do.

The Rock Crusher deconstructs the role of the classical product owner into its seven constituent roles. Roles are categorized as accountable, responsible, or supporting.

Accountable Roles

- *Backlog Owner.* The backlog owner has the final say on sequencing and prioritizing rocks for a team, and is accountable for ensuring the team is always working on the most valuable rocks.

- *Solution Owner.* The solution owner is a customer-facing role accountable for choosing (but not prioritizing) the rocks that make it into a solution.

Responsible Roles

- *Analyst.* An analyst is responsible for transforming input from the other village members into a shared, clear understanding of precisely what to build: the solution.

- *Team.* Team members are responsible for collaborating with all roles to decide precisely what to build. They are also accountable for delivering on their commitments to the backlog owner.

Supporting Roles

- *Customer.* The customer receives or benefits from the solution and may be consulted or informed about decisions on precisely what to build. Customers may also be stakeholders.

- *Stakeholder.* A stakeholder is anyone who at a minimum must be consulted about precisely what is being built, and who may have decision-making authority.

- *Subject Matter Expert* (SME). An SME uses deep knowledge of the relevant problem domain, technology, or development practices to advise other roles on deciding precisely what to build and to provide expertise that other roles may need to perform their jobs.

The number of people required to perform these roles greatly depends on the size and context of the enterprise and the development environment. In a small, focused skunkworks-like environment it may be possible for a single person to play all seven roles as the classical all-in-one product owner. In large, complex environments, each role may be occupied by several different people, each covering a particular subject or knowledge area. The notable exception to this is the backlog owner: This role is always held by a single person because we need a single voice for flow and accountability.

The final role in the village is the *team*: a group of individuals who are working together on a solution and can commit to pulling ready rocks through the thin pipe to deliver a solution increment. Commit in this context means the team has reasonable confidence they can execute and deliver the value described by the rock's intent in a predictable manner—either within an agreed timebox such as an iteration, or in keeping with a service level agreement (SLA).

Most of this book implies a small team the size of a typical Scrum or XP team (7 plus or minus 2), but the Rock Crusher model works for all teams, big or small. Using the Rock Crusher with large teams or a team of teams does not require any new roles. Chapter 14 The Rock Crusher at Scale provides guidance for scaling the Rock Crusher to larger groups.

Backlog Refinement

Refinement is an analysis and design process that shapes poorly formed rocks into well-formed rocks and splits larger abstract rocks into smaller, more concrete rocks. Refinement is first and foremost a learning process. It adds new knowledge and increases our understanding of the problem and of potentially valuable solutions. Refinement may also involve progressively splitting larger rocks into smaller rocks until they are sufficiently right-sized for pulling through the thin pipe.

Figure 2.7: Large, abstract rocks are refined into smaller, more concrete rocks

The Backlog Refinement Meeting

The classical backlog refinement meeting is an essential Rock Crusher ceremony. During a backlog refinement meeting, the team collaboratively analyzes and splits rocks. Backlog refinement with the Rock Crusher involves asking four questions about a rock:

- How valuable is this rock?
- How big is this rock?
- Is this rock worth it?
- How ready is this rock?

The answers to these questions help determine the rock's priority, subsequent refinement needs, and the urgency of creating a well-formed and ready rock.

The team may be able to refine many of the rocks during the refinement meeting itself. Other rocks may require significant investigation and analysis. The team may add crushers to the backlog to capture and manage this work. During the refinement meeting, the lessons from previous crushers are evaluated and used to guide subsequent refinement decisions and prioritization.

Crushers

Figure 2.8: Crushers make deciding precisely what to build visible and manageable

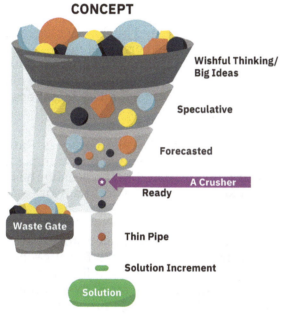

A *crusher* is simply a rock used to help refine other rocks. This special rock makes visible the learning activities which are present in the backlog refinement process. Crushers in the backlog are visual representations of the important analysis work required to properly refine a rock.

Just like any other rock, a crusher has an intent—which in this case is learning the knowledge necessary for further rock refinement. That learning results in a testable verifiable model, such as a customer journey that can be demonstrated. Accepted crushers are presented at the iteration review, just like all other work accepted by the backlog owner.

Unlike other rocks, when a crusher's verifiable model is accepted by the backlog owner, it does not become a solution increment. Rather, the accepted verifiable model represents what was learned about the rock we are trying to refine. The crusher creates economic value by reducing the risk of building the wrong thing and aligning the team on the ultimate solution. The crusher also represents work performed by members of the team and it may have a cost in terms of team capacity.

Crushers are not a justification for a stealth BUFD (big up-front design) process. Rather, they are intended to flow the work for deciding precisely what to build and to make that flow visible and manageable. The refinement work encapsulated in the crusher has a cost in one form or another, and this helps establish accountability for that work demanded from the team.

Crushers are similar to what many developers call a spike—a timeboxed story that answers a question. We chose the term *crusher* for two reasons: First, it fits our rock crushing metaphor. Second, and more importantly, the spike term is well entrenched in the agile community and usually refers to a technical exploration story. We want to broaden the scope of the learning to include the analysis and design processes.

Implementing the Rock Crusher with Kanban

Figure 2.9: Using a Kanban to implement the Rock Crusher

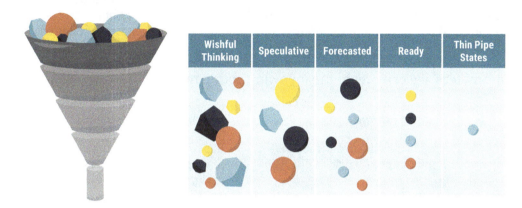

Most agile lifecycle management tools are primarily intended to serve as work management and reporting tools. They follow the stacked plates model to represent the backlog, which makes visualizing and managing the exploration difficult. However, the Rock Crusher can be approximated using a kanban board.

Kanban is an ideal tool for implementing the Rock Crusher because Kanban visualizes work and, by effectively limiting work in progress, enables us to manage throughput. Chapter 15 Implementing Your Rock Crusher presents several ways for using Kanban to represent the Rock Crusher.

Handling Rocks on and off the Roadmap

The Rock Crusher as described is a good tool to help us to visualize a roadmap of known rocks that might flow through a backlog. However, some, even most, of the team's work may not be planned and roadmapped rocks. We must supplement the Rock Crusher to account for this unplanned work.

Whether a rock is on our roadmap or not, it flows through the team's Rock Crusher funnel. The backlog owner cannot escape accountability for prioritizing all the rocks in the backlog—not just the roadmapped rocks. We have developed a strategy matrix for classifying and coping with rocks using two parameters, *expected* and *planned*.

- *Expected* rocks are probable work—the team knows the rock is coming, but may not be certain of when it will arrive. In contrast, *unexpected* rocks have a low probability of occurring; literally, the team does not expect them to happen.

- *Planned* rocks are known either because they're on the roadmap—explicitly planned—or because historical patterns have taught the team to plan for that work. *Unplanned* rocks are not on a roadmap and are not part of the team's historical patterns. Unplanned rocks can disrupt flow.

Using these parameters, we can create the following action matrix.

	Planned (known	Unplanned (unknown
Expected (high probability	This is classical roadmapped Rock Crusher work.	Based on historical patterns, the team regularly receives these rocks and they are managed using capacity allocation. This rock is not on the roadmap, but the team anticipates it.
Unexpected (low probability)	Although the team does not expect this rock, there is some (low) chance it will be needed. The team will have a plan for it, just in case. This is the domain of risk mitigation.	This is typically a crisis or black swan event. The team's only recourse for dealing with this rock is to break the thin pipe, abandon their commitment, deal with the event, and then retrospect to understand what happened.

Readiness Horizons

We suggest four readiness horizons—Ready, Forecasted, Speculative, and Wishful Thinking. These are only guides to suggest the possible scope, granularity, and urgency of different rocks. The exact meaning of these horizons depends on your organization's context. For example, the readiness horizon for Forecasted may be the next sprint for a small product development team or the next quarter for a very large program.

Here's what the Rock Crusher readiness horizons may mean for a small product development team:

- *Wishful Thinking / Big Ideas.* Typically represents anything in the far-off future, at least two or three quarters out. Flow is turbulent: The rocks are poorly formed and likely to change frequently, and are only moderately defined. It is not even certain if the rock will pass vetting. The rock's scope could be very large. It is unlikely the team can size the rock beyond a coarse T-shirt sizing (S, M, L). These rocks are "pitchable" but not yet defensible.

- *Speculative.* Flow is less turbulent but with only a moderate degree of certainty that all or part of the rock will be needed or will get done (e.g., a moderate to large epic user story). Rocks here may represent about a few weeks of work for a team. We do not expect to pull these rocks through the thin pipe for at least one or two months. The team can likely size the rock using finer T-shirt sizing (XS, S, M, L, XL). Some economic justification exists for the rock.

- *Forecasted.* Flow is significantly smoothed. Rocks are more well formed and near ready. There may be a fair amount of certainty that we will commit to the rock in a couple of weeks, or at most a couple of months. The rock is sufficiently well formed that a team can reasonably size it and know if they need to split it into right-sized rocks (can be implemented in a single iteration or sprint). Rocks are "near forced rank" prioritized.

- *Ready.* These rocks are ready for a team (e.g., a well-formed user story including acceptance criteria). Each rock is well formed and the right size for a team to commit to delivering it within an agreed timebox (e.g., an iteration or a SAFe® Program Increment). In a Kanban world, the team can satisfy their SLA for a rock of this type and size. Ready backlog rocks are prioritized by forced ranking.

Rock Crusher Metrics

How do you know the Rock Crusher is working? We recommend using value stream metrics to describe the Rock Crusher's performance. Mik Kersten's Flow Framework®[1] (flowframework.org) provides excellent metrics for understanding the health of the value stream.

Value stream thinking usually implies that all rocks entering the value stream get done. This may be close to the truth for manufacturing, but it certainly should not be the case in solution development. What goes in must come out, but it can come out through either the thin pipe or the waste gate. This creates a metric we call the *crush ratio*. Metrics are discussed in detail in Chapter 13 Is It Working? Rock Crusher Metrics.

Summary

- The Rock Crusher captures and visualizes the ambiguity that should be inherent in a backlog.
- The thin pipe is a metaphor for the team's limited capacity to deliver solution increments. The effectiveness of the thin pipe relies on a steady flow of ready rocks (backlog items).
- Rock Crusher flow is turbulent, and the purpose of the Rock Crusher is to make the processes and work of smoothing that flow visible and manageable.
- The waste gate is an important part of the model and explicitly demonstrates that not all rocks in the backlog will be pulled through the thin pipe.
- The Rock Crusher model acknowledges the difficulty of the product owner role and breaks it into a village of roles—backlog owner, solution owner, analyst, SME, stakeholder, and customer.
- A rock is a backlog item. A well-formed rock has an intent and results in a test-able verifiable model.
- What goes in must come out, either through the thin pipe or the waste gate. As with a traditional backlog, there is no commitment to a rock just because it is in the Rock Crusher. Rocks do not have to be fully refined, or even refined at all.

1. Kerten, M. *Project to Product: How to Survive and Thrive in the Age of Digital Disruption with the Flow Framework.* IT Revolution Press. 2018.

Try This

Try using the Rock Crusher to understand your workflow and your current backlog:

The Funnel
- Can you identify steps or ceremonies where you are, or should be, throttling flow (that is, reducing demand to balance it with the team's capacity to deliver)?
- Can you identify steps or ceremonies where you are or should be stabilizing the flow (that is, force ranking backlog items)?

The Thin Pipe
- Can you identify your thin pipe and the backlog items in the thin pipe? These would be the work that is ready for the team.
- Do you see any of these signs that the thin pipe is clogged or is clogging up?
  - The backlog of ready work is growing.
  - The team is experiencing "hangovers"—that is, work that was pulled and committed in a specific iteration is rolling over into the next and even subsequent iterations. Hangovers indicate that either the work items are too large or too much work is being forced through the thin pipe, exceeding the team's capacity.

The Waste Gate
- How and when are stories, features, and other backlog items removed from your backlog? Can the team remove backlog items, or does removal require administrative authority?

The Village
- Can you identify your backlog owner and solution owner? Are they the same individual or different individuals?

Readiness Horizons
- Is most of your team's work on your roadmap (planned and expected) or does it arrive randomly (unplanned and expected)? Are you frequently surprised by black swans—unplanned and unexpected work?

3   Rock Crusher Roles and Responsibilities

Learning Objectives

- Explain why, except for a small team, it's unrealistic to ask a single individual to fulfill the product owner role.
- Explain all the roles a product owner really plays.

Many parents are familiar with the expression "it takes a village to raise a child." This is also a good metaphor for deciding precisely what to build. Contrast this with classical agile methodologies that suggest a single individual can do everything.

According to the Scrum Guide:

> *The Product Owner is also accountable for effective Product Backlog management, which includes:*
>
> • *Developing and explicitly communicating the Product Goal;*
>
> • *Creating and clearly communicating Product Backlog items;*
>
> • *Ordering Product Backlog items; and,*
>
> • *Ensuring that the Product Backlog is transparent, visible, and understood.*
>
> *The Product Owner may do the above work or may delegate the responsibility to others. Regardless, the Product Owner remains accountable.*[1]

The product owner role, or any similar role such as the XP customer representative, is arguably the critical success factor for an agile team. You may be working with an amazing team of engineers who can craft brilliant code—build the system right—but the

---

1. Schwaber, K., and Sutherland, J. *The Scrum Guide.* 2020.

product owner is still accountable for the economic success of the product—building the right system. Many of the challenges agile teams encounter can be traced back to an unavailable, disengaged, or indecisive product owner.[1]

Recognizing that the value stream does not begin and end with the product owner stretches the classic product owner role to the point of ripping it into its constituent roles. It's unrealistic to assume a single omnipotent and omniscient individual can fully engage with a team while remaining connected to the market, especially at the enterprise scale. While the Scrum Guide does say the product owner "may do the above work or may delegate the responsibility," it does not provide guidance for how.[2] This model makes the backlog a reservoir of requirements and the product owner a glorified project manager. The team may gain technical agility, but the organization loses out on the economic benefit of product agility.

The Rock Crusher village deconstructs the omnipotent, omniscient product owner role into its seven constituent roles:

- Backlog Owner

- Solution Owner

- Analyst

- Subject Matter Expert (SME)

- Team

- Stakeholder

- Customer

People commonly occupy more than one role in a production—singer/songwriter, actor/director, writer/producer, player/coach, the list goes on. Similarly, the village describes roles and not individual job descriptions. As in any production, one individual may occupy multiple roles. For example, it would not be unusual for the backlog owner to also be an SME and an analyst. Except for the backlog owner, some of the village roles can also be fulfilled by multiple individuals: on a larger initiative, for example, multiple individuals may fulfill the analyst role in different domains.

How many individuals are involved in deciding precisely what to build depends on many factors such as the size and complexity of the solution, the size of the team, and

1. McDonald, K. *When Product Ownership Goes Bad*. Inside Product, November 9, 2017. https://insideproduct.co/when-product-ownership-goes-bad/.

2. Schwaber, K., and Sutherland, J. *The Scrum Guide*. 2020.

the nature of the market (mass market or contract). The main constraint is that the backlog owner for a given backlog is restricted to one individual. Scaling will require multiple individuals to play ownership roles, of course, but the rules of delegation ensure that there is always only one voice and one line of content ownership.

We use the RACI classifications to explain the relationships between the roles of the Rock Crusher village.

> RACI (Responsible, Accountable, Consulted, Informed) is a model of responsibility assignment and describes various roles in completing tasks or deliverables.
>
> • Responsible (R): the persons who will be performing the work on the task.
>
> • Accountable (A): the person who is ultimately held accountable for successful completion of the task and is the decision maker. Only one stakeholder receives this assignment.
>
> • Consulted (C): the stakeholder or stakeholder group who will be asked to provide an opinion or information about the task. This assignment is often provided to the subject matter experts (SMEs).
>
> • Informed (I): a stakeholder or stakeholder group that is kept up to date on the task and notified of its outcome. Informed is different from Consulted as with Informed the communication is one-direction (business analyst to customer) and with Consulted the communication is two-way.[1]

Accountable Roles

Ownership implies accountability, and the Rock Crusher's two ownership roles, *backlog owner* and *solution owner*, are both value management roles accountable for value delivery. The backlog owner is accountable for managing and maximizing the value delivered by the team. The solution owner is accountable for managing and maximizing the value created by the solution.

Backlog Owner

The backlog owner has the final say about the sequencing and prioritization of rocks for a team. The individual in this role is accountable for ensuring that the team is always working on the most valuable rocks. The backlog owner collaborates with all other roles (including the team) to make the best-informed decisions for prioritizing rocks for the team.

---

1. International Ins titute of Business Analysis (IIBA). A *Guide to the Business Analysis Body of Knowledge (BABOK® Guide)*, v. 3. 2015.

We chose the term backlog owner rather than continuing with the classical term product owner because we wanted to clearly differentiate the ownership roles. The individual nominated as the product owner is often really a solution owner and ignores their backlog ownership responsibility. The term backlog owner underscores that the individual playing this role is accountable for all the rocks in the backlog—not only rocks associated with growing the solution but also any transactional rocks in the backlog, such as defects and refactorings.

A fundamental principle of the Rock Crusher is that the team has limited capacity to pull rocks through the thin pipe and deliver value, whether as a solution increment or by completing transactional rocks. Therefore, the backlog owner is accountable for ensuring the team pulls the most valuable rocks through the thin pipe.

In the simplest collaborations, one individual can play both the backlog owner and solution owner roles, simplifying these prioritization decisions. In more complex ownership collaborations, such as when there are multiple solution owners, the backlog owner will need to decide between the competing demands to ensure the team is not overwhelmed while delivering the best overall value for the organization.

Solution Owner

The solution owner is a customer-facing role accountable for the features of a solution but does not have the final say regarding the prioritization of rocks for an individual team. A solution owner must collaborate with a backlog owner to get their features into the solution.

Our use of the term *feature* does not imply any kind of content management hierarchy or chunking mechanism. We mean features as defined by IIBA: a "distinguishing characteristic of a solution that implements a cohesive set of requirements and which delivers value for a set of stakeholders."[1]

Scrum assumes the product owner is available and interested in attending Scrum ceremonies, and will help explain backlog items and be available regularly to accept completed work. Somehow, between Scrum ceremonies and working with individual team members, the product owner must still have time to also be part of the business, understand the market, and decide what solution to build.

---

1. International Institute of Business Analysis. A *Guide to the Business Analysis Body of Knowledge (BABOK® Guide)*. version 3. 2015.

The typical reality is that many individuals nominated for the product owner role are primarily business people with little or no technical knowledge. Their interests are outward-facing; they are more concerned with what the customers really want from the solution, and prefer to defer technical innovation and implementation details to the technical team.

This leaves the team with a gap: Who will make the key decisions about these technical details? This is why we differentiate the roles of the solution owner and the backlog owner.

The solution owner:

- Is more outward-facing and customer oriented
- Typically takes a strategic view and owns a solution roadmap
- Is accountable for the value created by the solution

The backlog owner:

- Is more inward-facing and technology oriented
- Takes a tactical view and is accountable for all the rocks in the backlog
- Is responsible for maximizing the value delivered by the team
- Ensures the team is not starved and accepts their work

Naturally, the interests of the solution owner and backlog owner need to be aligned; otherwise, there is a potential for conflict.

As you can see, the backlog owner has a responsibility to the overall enterprise. Not all the rocks in the backlog may be directly related to a solution owner's solution or their solution roadmap. Some of the rocks are likely not on any roadmap but are instead necessary for the health and well-being of the overall enterprise, such as routine maintenance and patches. The greater a team's operational or support responsibilities, the likelier it is that these unplanned rocks will surface and conflicts will occur.

By explicitly distinguishing between the solution owner and backlog owner roles, we are attempting to force this conflict into the light where it can be handled correctly in the enterprise.

This collaboration between the solution owner and backlog owner is a fairly common pattern seen in many organizations. The outward-facing role is often called the product manager, and the inward-facing product owner works with the team on a daily basis.

Some variants of this model distinguish this collaboration by whether the individual comes from the business side of the organization (product managers or business product owners) or the technology side (product owners or technical product owners).

The Rock Crusher does not distinguish between individuals in the business and those in technology. Everyone is in the business. Without the technology there would be no business, and without the business there would be no reason for the technology.

The backlog owner–solution owner collaboration can get more complex and accountability can become cloudy when multiple solution owners collaborate with the backlog owner. Ideally these interests are well aligned, such as when several solution owners are evolving tightly related solutions, but we do see conflict between the incentives of the different roles all too frequently. Backlog owners and solution owners should actively work toward cooperation and alignment.

Some organizations set up specialty teams (UX designers, Cobol programmers), turning development teams into functional service provider teams and creating a situation ripe for conflict. This arrangement forces solution owners to compete for a scarce resource, which can encourage destructive conflicts between multiple solution owners, all of which must be resolved by the team's backlog owner.

To avoid this, we—like many agile experts—advocate for organizing teams around value streams and providing each team with the necessary skill sets to advance their product. When each team is independently able to achieve its goals, these types of conflicts are reduced or even eliminated.

Responsible Roles

Where accountable roles are expected to see that the work is completed, responsible roles are expected to actually do the work.

Analyst

An analyst is a team member responsible for transforming the sometimes competing wants, hopes, interests, and aspirations of the customer, stakeholder, and solution owner—as well as the contributions of the subject matter expert—into a shared, clear understanding of precisely what to build: the solution. The analyst role includes business analysts, requirements engineers, systems analysts, and other analysis roles.

Many organizations eliminated analyst roles in their rush to adopt agile as a development cost-reduction strategy. In the minds of many, the product owner role made analysts redundant. Unfortunately, many organizations that followed this path were soon harshly reminded of why the analyst role emerged in the first place. This is another example of overloading the product owner role with too many responsibilities.

BABOK® Guide defines business analysis as "the practice of enabling change in an enterprise by defining needs and recommending solutions that deliver value to stakeholders. Business analysis enables an enterprise to articulate needs and the rationale for change, and to design and describe solutions that can deliver value."[1]

The analyst role exists whether or not someone carries a business card with that title. As *BABOK® Guide* explains, "business analysts are responsible for discovering, synthesizing, and analyzing information from a variety of sources within an enterprise, including tools, processes, documentation, and stakeholders."[2]

From a Rock Crusher point of view, the analyst is a boundary-spanning role[3] collaborating with all other Rock Crusher roles. Each of these roles may have different views of the solution or use different terminology, and all will need to collaborate in order to quickly decide on precisely what to build.

The analyst's purpose is to increase knowledge and understanding across roles. They may do this via conversations, workshops, documents, visual models, and other collaborative activities. Analysts will sometimes use crushers to make visible the work they need to create the knowledge required to guide the refinement of a rock.

There are three common collaborations between the analyst and other Rock Crusher roles:

- *Analyst with Solution Owner.* One or more analysts may work with the solution owner to refine rocks for the solution. The analyst may also advise the solution and backlog owners on prioritization trade-offs and negotiations.

- *Analyst with Backlog Owner.* One or more analysts may work with the backlog owner to help them refine rocks in the backlog. When an individual fulfills this role, it is important that other team members do not abdicate responsibility for refining rocks. Many authors have suggested this pairing when the nominated business product owner is not fully available, with the analyst stepping in as the proxy product owner or the business product owner's

1. International Institute of Business Analysis. *A Guide to the Business Analysis Body of Knowledge (BABOK® Guide).* version 3. 2015.

2. IBID.

3. Nochur, K., and Allen, T. *Do Nominated Boundary Spanners Become Effective Technological Gatekeepers? (Technology Transfer).* IEEE Transactions on Engineering Management 39, no. 3 (August 1992). https://doi.org/10.1109/17.156560.

lieutenant. This pairing may be analogous to the solution owner–backlog owner pairing. The key differentiator is that the analyst is not accountable for value delivered by the team.

- *Analyst with Team Member.* An analyst is a team member who works with other team members to pull ready rocks through the thin pipe. In a software team, the analyst may work with a programmer, a tester, or a UX expert to get a rock done and deliver a solution increment. A simple example is team members working together on a complex financial algorithm, where the analyst can help inform the programmer and tester of the specifications for the algorithm.

Most agile methodologies do not explicitly acknowledge the analyst role; they usually imply that this function is owned by the product owner and performed in collaboration with the team. However, the analyst role emerged for a reason and is often filled by a designated individual. Having a dedicated analyst does not preclude the backlog owner or the team doing their own analysis work, and does not prevent the analyst from participating in other team roles. Agile teams have one very simple rule when it comes to roles: You do whatever is necessary to help your team get the job done.

The Team

Team members are responsible for collaborating with all roles to decide precisely what to build, and are accountable for delivering on their commitments to the backlog owner.

The stacked plates visualization of the backlog implies that the team is just a consumer of ready work, with minimal responsibilities during backlog refinement. In the Rock Crusher model, the team (we prefer this term to *developers*) is an active participant in backlog refinement. This goes straight back to the Agile Manifesto value statement regarding "customer collaboration over contract negotiations." The team actively and purposely collaborates with other Rock Crusher roles to decide precisely what to build. This is why we encourage placing the backlog at the center of the team rather than to the left as if it were a passive reservoir.

Although roles such as the solution owner and backlog owner are accountable for deciding precisely what to build, they are not dictatorial gatekeeper roles. Team members contribute their knowledge to refinement. The Rock Crusher village gains two significant advantages from this collaborative refinement process:

- They can make better refinement decisions because they are drawing on multiple sources of knowledge from multiple points of view.

- The team becomes so knowledgeable about the rocks they are refining that they can make believable delivery commitments to the backlog owner.

The Dangers of Disconnected Teams

As we have mentioned, one of the problems with the stacked plates backlog model is that it encourages the team to be coding-centric and may disconnect the team from the problem domain. This can happen when teams are treated as mere functional steps, like coding. Dropping a backlog between business and technology perpetuates this model and breaks the value stream. In the words of Fuller and Kruchten:

> It is important that everyone on the development team has a deep domain understanding and it is critical that everyone understands it in a compatible and consistent way. The reason is that team members (individually, in subteams, and across all functional roles) make decisions continually throughout product design and development. Indeed, they make decisions continually throughout the entire product life cycle, based on their individual understanding of the context of the requirements, and much of that context understanding is tacit.[1]

Without a deep, shared understanding of the problem domain, team members will make expedient decisions based on what they believe are the appropriate needs and trade-offs. The Rock Crusher's village model blurs the boundaries between roles throughout the value stream to deliver a solution that is better suited for its purpose.

How Big Is a Team?

Many of our graphics and examples imply a team organized like a small Scrum team of perhaps 5 to 11 people. The Rock Crusher does not prescribe team size or how the team is organized beyond prescribing that the team must collaborate with a backlog owner and a solution owner. The team's size and organization should be drawn from whatever agile framework the team chooses to use to inform their way of working. In chapter 14, we provide guidance for using the Rock Crusher with larger teams, which you can incorporate into your agile framework.

Supporting Roles

Supporting roles represent roles that must be either informed or consulted by the backlog owner. Customers, stakeholders, and SMEs all may need to be consulted or informed as rocks are refined and the solution emerges. Some of these roles may overlap.

---

1. Fuller, R., and Kruchten, P. *Blurring Boundaries: Toward the Collective Empathic Understanding of Product Requirements.* Information and Software Technology 140, no. 106670 (December 1, 2021). https://doi.org/10.1016/j.infsof.2021.106670.

The *customer* receives or benefits from the solution. They may need to be informed of the decision about precisely what the team will build.

A *stakeholder* is any individual who, at a minimum, must be consulted about precisely what is being built. Stakeholders may also have decision-making authority regarding the building process. A customer may also be a stakeholder if they need to be consulted regarding decisions about the solution.

A *subject matter expert* or *SME* is someone with in-depth knowledge of the relevant problem domain, solution technology, or development practices. SMEs use their knowledge to advise other roles about deciding precisely what to build. They are also responsible for providing the expertise other roles may need to perform their jobs.

While SMEs can collaborate with all roles, they typically tend to advise solution owners, analysts, and backlog owners.

Summary

- It is unreasonable to expect a single individual to effectively fulfill the responsibilities of the traditional product owner in all but the smallest of teams.
- The Rock Crusher village model highlights that backlog management requires the effective collaboration of seven roles: backlog owner, solution owner, analyst, SME, stakeholder, customer, and team.
- Effective backlog management and product delivery requires all roles to fully understand the domain.

Try This

- If you have a product owner, is that individual truly responsible for the backlog? Are they truly empowered to make backlog decisions? Do they optimize for overall value or are they only interested in their pet solution?
- Can you identify who is in your Rock Crusher village? Who in your enterprise plays each Rock Crusher role?
- Does your team have enough domain knowledge to contribute effectively to backlog refinement?

4   The Challenges of the Ownership Roles

Learning Objectives

- Explain why the Rock Crusher explicitly distinguishes the roles of backlog owner and solution owner.
- Explain the consequences of misaligned priorities between the backlog owner and solution owners.
- Explain how the analyst role moderates the relationship between the backlog owner and solution owners.
- Select the best of the three ownership models for your organization to encourage alignment and coordination between the ownership roles.
- Describe a metaphor for collaboration between a backlog owner and a subject matter expert that can help mitigate conflict between these roles.

When we developed the village model, we chose to call out two ownership roles based on the patterns of ownership we were observing: a backlog owner who owns the backlog and a solution owner who owns the solution. Many individuals who play the role of product owner are only interested in a fraction of the work in the backlog. To keep the Rock Crusher running smoothly and consistently, successfully delivering maximum value to the organization, the backlog owner and solution owners must be aligned. In this chapter we explore this important collaboration and describe three ownership models we have observed that can keep these ownership roles aligned.

This chapter also provides a model that can help moderate a sometimes contentious "near ownership" relationship between the architect, who is a subject matter expert (SME) in the Rock Crusher village, and the backlog owner.

The Challenge of Misaligned Ownership

In theory, any number of solution owners may collaborate with a backlog owner; however, solution owners often have differing and even competing goals or incentives. In such cases, it can be challenging to align their priorities. Even in the best of cases, every additional solution owner increases the risk of competition for scarce team resources. In extreme cases, solution owners may even go behind the back of the backlog owner or undercut other solution owners to achieve their own goals. One team member caught in this unfortunate dynamic, lamenting the dysfunction in his supposedly textbook agile team, described it to us this way: "Their priorities are not my priorities."

This is the misaligned ownership problem. The solution owners and the backlog owner are not aligned and are either unaware of the misalignment or hoping that the team can somehow resolve it for them.

The Rock Crusher attempts to address this problem in three ways:

- Establish clear ownership. The backlog owner owns the entire backlog, not just the part that interests them. They have the final say—both the responsibility to make wise choices and the authority to do so—on all rocks in the backlog.

- Make possible conflicts of ownership visible. Making these situations visible makes the team aware that a resolution must be achieved.

- Provide opportunities to resolve ownership conflicts. Refinement meetings for competing solution owners enable negotiation and resolution of conflicting priorities rather than solution owners abdicating their role and dumping that decision onto the team.

What the Rock Crusher cannot do is resolve malice and capriciousness. No set of engineering or product management practices can do that. If individuals wish to use positional authority and belligerence to get their way, then no process can keep them from choosing to misbehave. All we can do is make the dysfunction visible and show what such pathological behavior is costing the enterprise in terms of opportunities. As Alistair Cockburn once remarked, "People trump process."[1] In consulting, we sometimes have to tell a client: "It's your foot. Shoot it if you want to."

---

1. Cockburn, A., and Highsmith, J. *Agile Software Development: The People Factor*. Computer 34, no. 132. 2001. http://dx.doi.org/10.1109/2.963450.

Ownership Collaboration Models

We have observed three common and effective ownership collaboration patterns, or models:

- *Classical* – one individual playing both the backlog owner and solution owner roles.
- *Pairwise* – a single backlog owner collaborating with a single solution owner, with the solution owner typically taking a more outward-facing view with customers and stakeholders and the backlog owner a more inward-facing role with the team.
- *Cat herding* – a single backlog owner collaborating with multiple solution owners.

As far as multiple backlog owners with one or more solution owners: Don't do it! Don't! Just Don't!

Classical Model

The simplest ownership collaboration model is when the backlog owner and solution owner are the same person. This is the textbook agile approach to backlog management. Here, a fully empowered individual representing the business collaborates with a small, cross-functional, collaborative team. This individual sets solution direction, clarifies and prioritizes the backlog, and helps identify and clarify rocks. They accept the solution increments created by the team and are held accountable for value delivery.

The advantage of this model is there are no conflicting conversations about priorities and the value of the rocks (unless the product owner is conflicted). There is a single contact point for priorities and behavior. While both researchers and practitioners have expressed their reservations about the sustainability of this model, it can and does work—up to a certain level of scale or complexity.

The classical model can be sufficient for teams doing internal tool development, or for small, fast-moving product teams in a start-up, or for the small, fast, autonomous skunkworks team in a larger organization. This unified ownership model is simple, and as engineers like to say, simple is beautiful. Or as agilists are fond of saying, "Do the simplest thing that will work."

In one variation of the classical model, an analyst may handle some of the daily workload for the product owner. For example, the product owner may offload the responsibility for detailed discovery, analysis, synthesis, and writing backlog items to an analyst.[1] The unified ownership role is demanding, and offloading knowledge discovery, modeling, and rock refinement work helps make the role more sustainable.

This model works best when it enables the best decision-making speed and minimizes potential confusion over accountability. But it can cause problems in more complicated contexts. Simple is beautiful; simplistic is destructive.

Pairwise Model

Another common ownership model is pairwise collaboration between a more outward-facing solution owner and a more inward-facing backlog owner. This pattern also applies when multiple individuals play the role of the solution owner, but they all speak with one voice for one solution.

A major challenge with the classic product owner model is the expectation that the individual playing the product owner role is fully connected to the market or business needs and always available to work with the team. This model acknowledges that it is impossible for a single individual to stay connected to both the market and the business in most situations. Many individuals nominated as product owners have day jobs in product management, focusing on customers and the marketplace. In these cases, either product management or backlog management—and ultimately both—will suffer.

In the pairwise model, the responsibility for determining precisely what to build is a collaboration between a single solution owner and a single backlog owner. The solution owner maintains a big picture, product-centric, customer-facing view of the solution and drives the solution roadmap. The backlog owner works closely with the team to refine ready rocks and prioritizes which rocks the team should refine and pull through the thin pipe. Depending on the specific skills and domain expertise needed, an analyst may collaborate with the solution owner and/or the backlog owner to facilitate refinement of the rocks.

The pairwise model is common in product development organizations that have an outward-facing product management group. The product management group owns the solution and collaborates with the backlog owner and team to bring the product to market. Multiple product managers may work with the team; if they all speak with one voice for one product, they are effectively a single solution owner.

---

1. Leyton, R. *The Agile Business Analyst: Moving from Waterfall to Agile*. Leyton Publishing. 2015.

This model will fail if there is confusion surrounding accountability and decision-making authority. The solution owner is accountable for the value delivered by the solution and the backlog owner is responsible for the value created by the team. To avoid problems, both owners must ensure they remain aligned, collaborative, and in sync with the overall goals of the enterprise. If they do not, the enterprise—and very likely the team—will take the hit. This is where the analyst's facilitation skills come into play; the analyst is responsible for ensuring that all Rock Crusher village roles share a clear understanding of the backlog and the solution.

A solution owner may be highly engaged with the team, participating in sprint/iteration planning meetings and reviews while providing ongoing clarification of their needs. Or, the solution owner may be almost completely hands-off, only participating in midhorizon planning sessions such as release planning, and delegate most of the refinement responsibility to the backlog owner and team.

How hands-off the solution owner is depends on the trust relationship between the solution owner and backlog owner, as well as the domain and technical knowledge of each. If the backlog owner and team are knowledgeable in the solution domain, then a light touch by the solution owner may be best. If they are not, a light touch will lead to confusion and delays.

Cat Herder Model

A common scenario in more project-oriented organizations will have a team working on multiple solutions, each with its own solution owner. All the rocks for each of these different solutions flow turbulently through the Rock Crusher, and the backlog owner is accountable for deciding how to throttle and stabilize this turbulent flow. Even in the best situations the backlog owner will have to negotiate competing interests and priorities with the different solution owners while facilitating productive discussions.

As scale increases, the biggest risk is that the interests of the solution owners are not aligned. Lack of alignment leads to destructive competition and conflict. In the worst situations, some enterprises incentivize the solution owners to compete against each other and simply hope the backlog owner can figure it out. This is damaging to the team and likely to the overall goals of the enterprise. It will also likely encourage the departure of the backlog owner.

Figure 4.1: In the cat herder model, the backlog owner collaborates with multiple solution owners, serving as a facilitator and negotiator of value

When a backlog owner collaborates with multiple solution owners, negotiation and facilitation skills are crucial to success.

For this model to work, all participants need to understand the economics of flow. In many project-oriented organizations, the solution owners assume that if they have budget then the team has capacity. Solution owners often build roadmaps based on the "efficient utilization of resource capacity" rather than flowing work through the thin pipe. Anyone who commutes on a freeway that is "at capacity" knows this is a recipe for disaster.

All participants in this model need to be aware of the waste of task switching. Every time the team changes focus from rocks for one solution to rocks for another, they will incur a context switch penalty. This cost can be substantial—at least a 20% dip in productivity—and adds significant delay to solution delivery.

All participants in this model must also share a clear understanding of the enterprise goals. Maintaining flow and minimizing the waste of movement requires some economically rational way of prioritizing each solution owner's initiative. Everyone must be able to agree on an ordering of rocks that offers the enterprise the best economic outcome.

Finally, the backlog owner in this model needs great facilitation skills and must understand flow-based economics and Lean. There will be many times a backlog owner will need to explain to a solution owner why delaying implementation of the solution owner's pet initiative benefits them and the enterprise. Once again, this workload may be excessive for one person; if so, much of the load can be shared with one or more analysts.

The Analyst's Role

Analysis skills and subject matter expertise are implicit in these three collaboration models. Recall that a given person may play several roles, although one and only one person is permitted the role of backlog owner.

Analysts and SMEs can come from many business areas, with different backgrounds, knowledge, and domain expertise. Analysts help by making complex things simpler—or at least visible. SMEs help by contributing relevant knowledge that others do not have to inform positive decision-making.

Analyst skills are necessary in all types of product development, and become more important as collaborations expand, the number of individuals increases, and the scale of domains increases, for several reasons. First, many prioritization conflicts happen because people do not share a clear understanding of enterprise objectives and strategy beyond their own domain. The Rock Crusher analyst reconciles these conflicting perspectives such that the team has a fair chance at a principled and objective discussion of priorities.

Second, the analyst is often also an SME on the organization. Their knowledge of how the enterprise gets things done can help the backlog owner and solution owners make better prioritization decisions.

Third, discovering the knowledge needed to make objective prioritization decisions often requires significant work. This is the analyst's "sweet spot"—discovering and presenting that knowledge in a form everyone can understand and use.

Finally, great analysts have great facilitation skills, which may be called upon frequently in contentious meetings. These professionals also have skills in meeting facilitation, running workshops, managing problem backlogs, and more, increasing the efficiency and efficacy of group work activities.

Good Practice Ideas

As the enterprise scales, so do the challenges: the complexity of working with multiple solution owners, keeping their interests aligned, and spending team capacity in the best possible way to deliver the best possible economic outcome for the enterprise. The backlog owner, along with the analysts and SMEs, must work with solution owners to maximize value for the enterprise. Here are some good practice ideas that will give the team the best chance of driving the most valuable outcomes:

- Limit work in progress.

- Prioritize work that maximizes value for end customers.

- Be real about what is and is not aligned with the enterprise strategy.

- Estimate team capacity over the relevant release periods and plan the spend of that capacity across different time horizons.

- Reserve team capacity along the way for the usual non-roadmapped rocks such as patches, outages, and top-tier-client interruptions (see Chapter 9 Handling Rocks on and off the Roadmap).

- Ensure that the solution increments the team delivers are of the highest quality.

- Ensure the team adopts practices that ensure a sustainable pace.

- Reserve capacity for churn. For example, when a team member leaves, the team typically loses at least twice that person's capacity, because the remaining team members will have to train a replacement.

- Use the visibility created by the Rock Crusher and explain the economics of flow to reduce and mitigate political maneuvering, decisions by executive authority, and overriding the backlog owner—such actions typically draw capacity away from the team and reduce overall throughput and value creation.

When solution owners and the backlog owner collaborate on these items by sharing responsibility for success, the system functions at or near maximum throughput and creates the most value.

The Rock Crusher is about visibility because visibility contributes to success. Behaviors that contribute to success include being transparent with all stakeholders and keeping them well informed about the plan, risks, and progress.

SME and Backlog Owner Collaborations

Collaboration between the backlog owner and SMEs is challenging in many enterprises. Any sophisticated system requires significant technical work to realize a feature that is desirable to the customer and stakeholders, and much of this work is prioritized by the technical SMEs such as architects or systems engineers. This is why we sometimes say some SMEs have a "near ownership" role.

Organizations sometimes try to solve the problem of the product owner's lack of technical knowledge and lack of interest in technical priorities by having both a product owner and a technical product owner. We will say it again: Don't do this. Do not institutionalize multiple backlog owners for the same backlog. Unless you wish to institutionalize conflict and delay, only one person owns the backlog.

The problem many enterprises are trying to solve with multiple product owners is the product owner's lack of technical knowledge and lack of interest in technical priorities when making prioritization decisions. A product owner typically comes from the product management group and may not have a detailed understanding of the solution implementation. They need to lean heavily on technical SMEs for prioritization advice. In some situations, the product owner abdicates their product owner responsibility to an architect or other technical SME. This often results in an engineering-focused product that may not be fit for purpose.

One consequence of a strict engineering focus is that different stakeholder "thought worlds" can impede communication and coordination, and therefore new product development. For example, one study[1] describes the case of a manufacturing engineer who proudly demonstrated a keyboard's durability by tossing it against the wall. In his thought world, the engineer prized reliability and quality. Unfortunately, the product was a commercial failure—in part because the keyboard was too difficult to use. How often the keyboard could be thrown against a wall was not a factor in commercial success.

---

1. Dougherty, D. *Interpretive Barriers to Successful Product Innovation in Large Firms*. Organization Science, 3(2). 1992.

Thoughts from Steve

In enterprises where SMEs and backlog owners collaborate successfully, I have noticed a common pattern I call the Marine Pilot, after those expert mariners who guide ships to safety using their deep understanding of dangerous waterways. I live in a coastal city whose inlets and fjords are a ship graveyard. When a ship enters the local water, a marine pilot will board the ship and help guide the ship to port.

Both the ship's captain and the marine pilot are expert mariners. The main difference between them is that the pilot is an expert in the local waterways. A marine pilot who boards a ship does not take command and never gives direct orders to the crew. Instead, the pilot gives recommendations to the captain, who then issues the orders. The captain can choose not to follow the pilot's recommendations if they believe they would put the ship at risk. Even with the pilot on board, the captain is still accountable for the safety of the vessel.

This relationship is a good metaphor for effective collaboration between the backlog owner and SMEs. The backlog owner is accountable for the value delivered by the team, and the SME, often an architect or systems engineer, is the pilot. Each respects the other's expertise, and both acknowledge that it is the captain's ship. In the end, it is the backlog owner's backlog, not the SME's.

The relationship between the captain and marine pilot works in part because they have similar backgrounds and understand each other's perspectives. When the backlog owner and SME have significantly different backgrounds, it is critical for each to learn and appreciate the other's role and value to the enterprise. It may help to have one individual shadow the other for a day or week. Some organizations institutionalize this shadowing practice with "walk a mile in someone else's shoes" programs.

Collaboration Is Key

Regardless of the domain, the complexity of the environment, or the nature of the work, collaboration among the ownership roles is key to successfully delivering value in product development. The backlog owner and solution owners must align on outcomes, agree on priorities, and avoid back-channel manipulation to enable the best outcomes for the organization.

Summary

- The enterprise will suffer economically if the individuals acting as backlog owner and solution owner are not aligned and cannot cooperate.
- The analyst, with their knowledge discovery skills, subject matter expertise, and facilitation skills, helps moderate the relationship between the backlog owner and solution owners.
- There are three models for an effective collaboration between ownership roles:
  - Classical model, where one individual fills both roles.
  - Pairwise model, with collaboration between a single backlog owner and a single solution owner.
- Cat herder model, where a single backlog owner collaborates with multiple solution owners.
- The Marine Pilot metaphor illustrates effective collaboration between the backlog owner and an SME.

Try This

- Who is your backlog owner and who is your solution owner? Which model best describes their current collaboration?
- How do your backlog owner and the solution owners resolve conflicting priorities in your organization?
- Is the relationship between your backlog owner and the SMEs like the relationship between a ship's captain and a marine pilot?
- How are disagreements between the backlog owner and SMEs resolved?
- What roles are your analysts playing in moderating these relationships?

The Challenges of the Ownership Roles

5 Correctly Defining and Managing Rocks

Learning Objectives

- Describe a well-formed rock.
- Explain why well-formed rocks are important.
- Describe how well-formed rocks contribute to the solution being built.
- Explain why many rocks should be discarded through the waste gate.
- List the consequences of pulling poorly formed rocks through the thin pipe.

Rock is just our word for a backlog item—any backlog item of value waiting to be implemented. While many frameworks categorize backlog items by size—for example, stories and epics—the Rock Crusher does not. Large or small, well formed or not, everything is just a rock. Rocks may require further refinement, or they may be ready to pull through the thin pipe to the team for delivery.

"Standards are wonderful, everyone should have one." This old engineering joke calls out the challenges created by the proliferation of proprietary and local standards. This is true in agile frameworks as well; different frameworks use a wide range of common, yet conflicting names to describe different types of backlog items. We do not want to place you in unintentional conflict with your chosen software development framework and its related terminology, so we decided to review some of these terms to help you avoid confusion as you read this book.

Figure 5.1: A rock is a rock is a rock

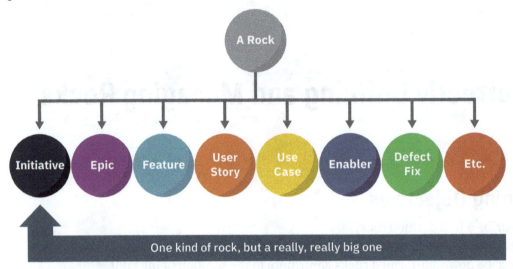

The following common terms are in broad and highly inconsistent use:

- *User story*. A small chunk of valuable work a team can generally complete within a short timebox (e.g., a sprint or iteration). Introduced as part of Extreme Programming, user stories, sometimes simply called "stories," are now widely used as a backlog item type. A well-formed user story consists of both a narrative and acceptance criteria.

- *Technical story*. Sometimes also called an "enabler." A technical story is generally a user story that does not deliver direct end-user value. It is often used to capture technical work that enables the direct delivery of user value. Common technical stories are environment or system patches, upgrades, architectural runway, or technical debt activity.

- *Epic*. Originally intended to represent a user story that was too big for a team to complete in a single timebox. Some frameworks have overloaded the term, using *epic* to refer to large-scale initiatives.

- *Feature*. One of the most overloaded terms in our industry, *feature* is often used to refer to valuable capabilities a product offers. Some frameworks also use features as a chunking mechanism; here, a feature becomes a bit like a user story's big sibling and represents a valuable service that can be completed by a large team of teams within a long timebox (e.g., one quarter). Some frameworks show the hierarchical structure as Epic-Feature-Story roughly showing the size of the different elements, while other frameworks show this hierarchy is shown as Feature–Epic–Story.

- *Capability*. Yet another overloaded term. For most business analysts, a capability represents a business function. Some frameworks use the term *capability* as a chunking mechanism to represent very large chunks of work.

- *Theme*. Sometimes a backlog item representing extremely large initiatives or programs; other times an overall strategy.

This is just a sampling of the inconsistent terminology in our industry. Worse, the backlog item terms in a team's methodology often differ from the terms used in their tooling. Just ask any organization using both SAFe® and Jira about the mental gymnastics they preform when using the term *epic*.

The Rock Crusher represents all backlog items as generic rocks. Of course, rocks vary in size and may or may not be well formed. Some of our colleagues have joked that their rocks are really mountains or even mountain ranges, but they are all just rocks to the Rock Crusher. Backlog items like user stories will be small in scope and much more concrete—pebbles and sand—but they are still just rocks.

Well-Formed Rocks

A well-formed rock is one for which we can explicitly demonstrate a valuable outcome. That valuable outcome may be anything from a model sketched on a whiteboard to a working solution increment.

A well-formed rock:

- is one for which we can clearly set expectations for what outcome should be delivered,

- results in a demonstrable and verifiable outcome, and

- the outcome can be tested to decide whether it is done correctly.

A well-formed rock has an intent, a verifiable model, and a test. The rock's *intent* describes the outcome we are seeking and aligns expectations. A rock's intent is realized (or implemented) by a *verifiable model*. Whether the verifiable model is a working solution increment, a simulation model, or a sketch on the whiteboard, a verifiable model can be demonstrated. The verifiable model is verified by a test. The test can be anything from a wonderful automated test suite for software to simply getting consensus agreement on a whiteboard sketch from colleagues.

Figure 5.2: A well-formed rock

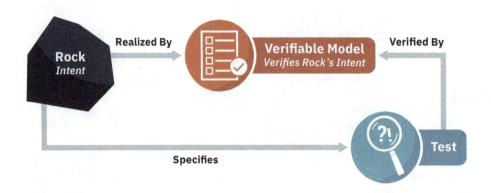

Identifying Well-Formed Rocks

What precisely is a well-formed versus not-so-well-formed rock depends somewhat on the context and the team's tacit knowledge. In simple, practical terms, well-formed means everyone shares a clear understanding of what needs to be done, when it will be done, and how to demonstrate that it has been done correctly. A tight team may need very little formal description of the rock's intent. Here are a few examples of how a team might judge different rocks.

> *As a Subscriber I need to update my location information so that I can be easily found.*
>
> *Acceptance Criteria*
> - *Verify location information can be updated from cell phone location data.*
> - *Verify Subscriber can disable automatic update of location information.*

This rock is a classic user story and is well formed. There is an intent ("I need to update my location information") and the acceptance criteria help scope the rock and create a test for the resulting verifiable model. "So that I can be easily found" explains why this story is valuable and can help the team create tests to verify that the verifiable model is fit for purpose.

> *Raise "keep alive" signal every 25 msec.*

Whether this rock is well formed or not depends on the team's tacit knowledge. Assuming the team knows what a keep alive signal is, how to raise one, and how to prove that it was emitted, then this may be an example of a well-formed rock.

Analyze automatic location update.

This is not a well-formed rock. Even if the team understands what it means, this is just a lazy task description with no indication of an intended outcome. There is nothing anyone could take to an iteration review and demonstrate as completed or learned.

When debating whether a rock is well formed or not, ask "What will we show at the review/demo to demonstrate that this rock is correctly done?" We use this question a lot during iteration planning meetings. It helps the team focus on the outcome of the rock rather than just the work.

In practical terms, a well-formed rock represents work a team can predictably pull through the thin pipe and objectively demonstrate as done. Pulling poorly formed rocks through the thin pipe—that is, rocks that are not ready—will quickly clog the thin pipe and ruin predictable delivery of value. If the rock's intent is not objectively clear, how can the team size the rock, plan with it, and commit to its delivery? How can the team know what external dependencies the rock may have? Poorly formed rocks are a root cause of many of the problems teams have with predictable delivery.

Right-Sizing Rocks

When it comes to rocks, size does matter. A rock may be well formed, but if it is too large to pull through the thin pipe it will clog it just as easily as a poorly formed rock. In the agile and Lean world, small is beautiful. Small, well-formed rocks will move through our system with greater speed and predictability than large, well-formed rocks.

Most agile frameworks right-size rocks based on whether they can be delivered within a known and standard period of time. For example, Scrum's timebox is a sprint, and rocks that are pulled into the sprint should be sized such that the team can commit to completing the rock within that sprint. Rocks which would require more than one sprint are not considered right-sized. Flow frameworks like Kanban use service level agreements (SLAs) and a relentless desire to reduce lead times to limit rock size.

Size alone does not define a poorly formed rock. A large, initiative-sized rock can be well formed if everyone is clear on the intent, the verifiable model, and the tests to demonstrate it. But we would never pull the entire initiative through the thin pipe. The whole purpose of the Rock Crusher is to reveal and manage the process for refining that large initiative into right-sized rocks that we can pull through the thin pipe.

Progressive Refinement

Most readers are probably familiar with hierarchical decomposition of backlog items: a large user story—sometimes called an epic—is decomposed, or split, into smaller child user stories. For example, a large user story or epic for cash withdrawal from an ATM may be broken down into several valuable child user stories for authenticating the ATM card, selecting the account, and dispensing cash.

Figure 5.3: Rocks too large to pull through the thin pipe should be split into smaller well-formed and right-sized rocks

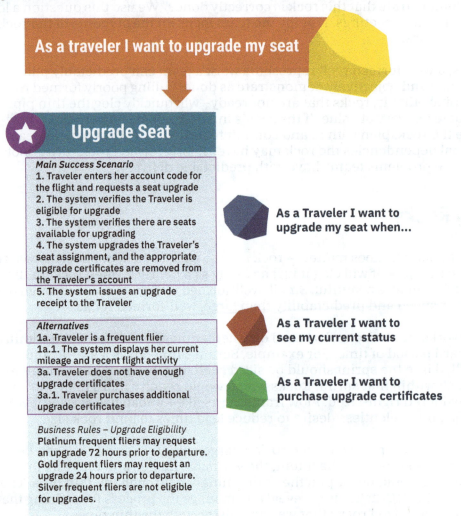

As a traveler I want to upgrade my seat

★ **Upgrade Seat**

Main Success Scenario
1. Traveler enters her account code for the flight and requests a seat upgrade
2. The system verifies the Traveler is eligible for upgrade
3. The system verifies there are seats available for upgrading
4. The system upgrades the Traveler's seat assignment, and the appropriate upgrade certificates are removed from the Traveler's account
5. The system issues an upgrade receipt to the Traveler

Alternatives
1a. Traveler is a frequent flier
1a.1. The system displays her current mileage and recent flight activity
3a. Traveler does not have enough upgrade certificates
3a.1. Traveler purchases additional upgrade certificates

Business Rules – Upgrade Eligibility
Platinum frequent fliers may request an upgrade 72 hours prior to departure. Gold frequent fliers may request an upgrade 24 hours prior to departure. Silver frequent fliers are not eligible for upgrades.

As a Traveler I want to upgrade my seat when...

As a Traveler I want to see my current status

As a Traveler I want to purchase upgrade certificates

We can enhance our model of a well-formed rock to reflect this parent-child hierarchy.

Figure 5.4: Expanded model of a well-formed rock

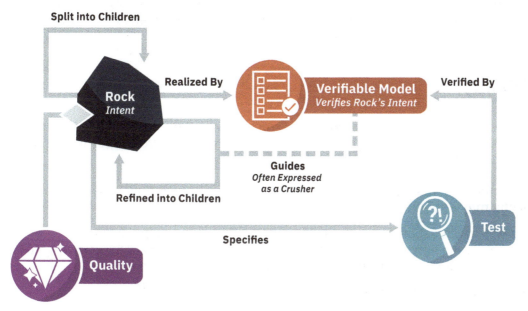

While this model may appear intimidating at first, it simply acknowledges the generational structural hierarchy of backlog items. Large, well-formed initiative-sized rocks (boulders or even mountains) are progressively decomposed into smaller well-formed rocks. Eventually, rocks are right-sized such that they can be pulled through the thin pipe without clogging it.

Progressive refinement of a large rock into smaller well-formed child rocks does not automatically result in a well-formed parent rock. Just because the parts are well formed does not mean the whole is well formed. The team may be able to demonstrate that the verifiable model for the child rocks satisfies their intent, but unless they are clear on the intent of the parent rock, they cannot know if the sum of the functions of the child rocks satisfies it. It is possible to build high-quality system components for an overall system that is not fit for purpose. This is why many frameworks have functional and user acceptance testing steps and do not simply declare victory because the software passed its unit tests.

Rocks rarely start out well formed. Even large initiative-sized rocks usually start out as a vague verb phrase on a card and need refinement. Much of what the Rock Crusher is about is managing the turbulent process for refining poorly formed rocks into well-formed ready rocks the team can pull through the thin pipe. By the time the team is ready to pull the rock through the thin pipe, it should be right-sized and its intent should be objectively clear to everyone.

Rock Quality

Quality is a constraint on the intent and describes how well the team has to implement the intent. Quality is crucial, so it is called out explicitly, and drives both the verifiable model and the test.

The team's mechanisms for specifying quality will vary. For a software system, any of the following may apply:

- System-wide nonfunctional requirements specifying system attributes such as performance, reliability, maintainability, or other factors. ISO standard 25010 (www.iso.org/standard/35733.html) has a useful list of quality characteristics for software.

- Accessibility and usability needs.

- Mean Time to Failure.

- Mean Time to Repair.

- Response time.

- Security boundaries and abilities.

If a software-construction backlog item includes quality constraints that need to be met for the rock to be considered done, it's good practice to maintain a Definition of Done describing the required level of completeness. But a quality constraint is not unique to software. All verifiable models, whether directly executable or not, need to be created to some level of quality to be useful.

Identifying quality constraints can be as challenging as identifying value; quality has many dimensions, and different stakeholders will have different quality needs, some of which may be contradictory. Trade-offs must be made. For instance, in a financial product the security group will need defined levels of access control, while the customer service group may want to reduce the number of service calls due to lost security credentials. Completely satisfying both groups may be impossible, so the team will need to facilitate conversations and build the appropriate security constraints and customer support needs into the quality criteria. Part of that facilitation process may require creating a crusher, or spike, to generate the learning needed to make an informed decision. (See chapter 6 for more on crushers.)

Discarding Rocks

Not all rocks will be valuable, in fact we expect many of the rocks that come into the Rock Crusher to be discarded through the waste gate. As was mentioned in chapter 2, the waste gate is a crucial element of the Rock Crusher; it enables flow and prevents the accumulation of zombie rocks. Part of the work of refining rocks is identifying those that are not worth working on and deliberately discarding them through the waste gate.

Verifiable Models, Solution Increments, and Solutions

Ideally, the rock's verifiable model becomes a solution increment when it is accepted by the backlog owner. A *solution increment* grows the *solution*, which represents some value-generating product or service for the enterprise. A solution could be a product or service offered for sale (a home router, an industrial image setter, a consumer subscription streaming service) or an enabler for services that the enterprise delivers to its customers (online banking, an online airline reservation system). A solution could be a nonprofit service, such as housing or free child care. It could even be something the enterprise is contracted to deliver, such as software.

Rocks are backlog items that are processed through the Rock Crusher to contribute to a solution that delivers value to the organization.

Figure 5.5: A rock's verifiable model becomes a solution increment when accepted by the backlog owner

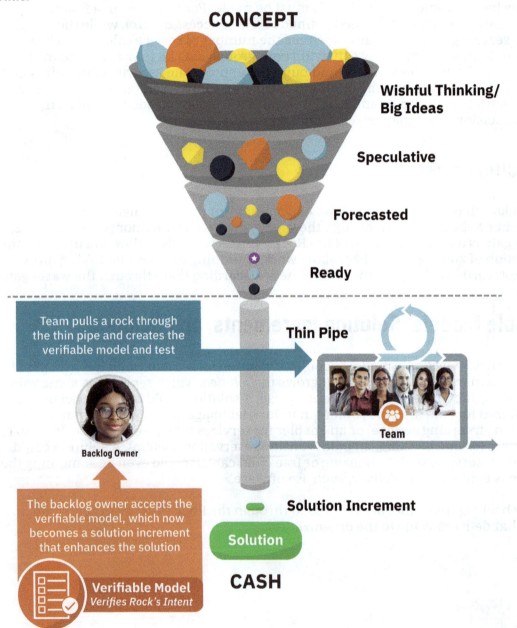

CONCEPT

Wishful Thinking/
Big Ideas

Speculative

Forecasted

Ready

Team pulls a rock through
the thin pipe and creates the
verifiable model and test

Thin Pipe

Team

Backlog Owner

The backlog owner accepts the
verifiable model, which now
becomes a solution increment
that enhances the solution

Solution Increment

Solution

Verifiable Model
Verifies Rock's Intent

CASH

Summary

- A rock is a backlog item. All backlog items in the Rock Crusher, regardless of methodology or team customs, are simply rocks.
- A well-formed rock expresses an intent which is implemented (realized) by a verifiable model. The verifiable model can be objectively tested (verified) with a test.
- Pulling poorly formed rocks through the thin pipe—that is, rocks that are not ready—will quickly clog the thin pipe and ruin predictable delivery of value.
- A solution is a value-creating asset for the organization. When the backlog owner accepts a rock's verifiable model, the verifiable model becomes a solution increment that enhances the solution.

Try This

- How many different terms—epic, feature, user story, theme—are used to describe backlog items in your organization?
  - Do these terms all have consistent definitions?
  - If you ask five people this question, will they all give you the same answer?
- Do your framework definitions and tools conflict?
- What are some examples of verifiable models in your organization? For a software development team, "working software" is the obvious answer, but do you create other work products to understand a backlog item, such as models?
- How do you demonstrate that your work products are correct or that you correctly understand the intent of a backlog item?
- Can you concisely describe the solution your team builds? Can your team?

Correctly Defining and Managing Rocks

6   Use Crushers to Make Analysis Visible

Learning Objectives

- Explain how crushers make learning precisely what to build visible and manageable.
- Describe how teams can use crushers to refine a backlog incrementally.
- Explain how the knowledge that we are all "model builders" can help us create better rocks.
- List the three verification levels that support progressive and incremental refinement of rocks.

Rocks typically start out poorly formed and are progressively refined into well-formed and right-sized rocks that can be pulled through the thin pipe. Sometimes a large effort is required to refine a poorly formed rock into well-formed and right-sized rocks.

Consider a typical scenario: a stakeholder asks the team to provide a new service. The team may have to expend significant effort to determine what problem the stakeholder wants to solve—in Fredrick Brooks' words, "deciding precisely what to build."[1] It may be a significant effort just to elicit the problem the stakeholder wants to solve. Yet more effort may be required to organize all the contradictory statements into a coherent intent. Then there may be considerable effort spent to discover how that intent could be implemented.

Good agile guidance is to deliver small, incremental feature slices of the system quickly. The team leverages its strong collaborative relationship with the stakeholder to frequently demonstrate production-quality feature slices. The stakeholder, always ready to answer questions, offers their feedback on the working software. The team

1. Brooks, F. *No Silver Bullet: Essence and Accidents of Software Engineering.* Computer 20, no. 4. 1987.

quickly determines whether the feature slice is fit for purpose and, by proxy, whether they are on the right track to creating a fit-for-purpose solution. They then use the learning to quickly refactor the system.

This process is often called emergent design—iteratively and incrementally, the stakeholder and the team learn what is needed. Frequent delivery of working software accelerates the feedback and learning cycle. This enables the team to discover what their stakeholders really want, not just what they say they want. The Agile Manifesto calls out "working software" because it is the gold standard for delivering a fit-for-purpose solution.

But sometimes we can't or shouldn't go for the gold. It may take significant effort to create any working software that stakeholders can offer helpful or worthwhile feedback on. The team may need to understand complex system interactions that are obscured by the working software. Relying on working software as the only measure of progress and learning can delay decision-making. Furthermore, many systems defy implementation feature slice by feature slice.

What is our alternative? A team following classical waterfall processes, or a hybrid agile process would refine the large rock up front, then pursue elicitation, analysis, design, and finally implementation. They would use gates such as preliminary design review and critical design review to verify their understanding of the problem and whether the proposed solution is fit for purpose. Eventually, the solution would be refined into a work breakdown structure of right-sized tasks that the team would begin executing. Even if this team uses agile practices—hybrid agile—the economic costs of delay will be high. Furthermore, there is a high risk of building a product that satisfies the requirements but is not fit for purpose.

In Homer's *Odyssey*, Odysseus and his men had to navigate a narrow, dangerous strait between two sea monsters: Scylla, who devoured sailors, and Charybdis, who created whirlpools that devoured ships. When it comes to analysis and design we seem to be stuck between the Scylla of emergent design and the Charybdis of big up-front design. Either we boldly, even recklessly, start implementing the system and hope a fit-for-purpose system emerges, or we delay implementation until all our documentation claims we understand precisely what to build. Then we hope the documented system is fit for purpose.

Hope is never a plan of action. We need a technique that will help us avoid these hazards altogether. With a system of any complexity, we need additional tools that enable us to navigate between "just code it" and "design it all up front."

Crushers—Rocks for Backlog Refinement

Mining provides us with a helpful mental model for visualizing and managing a flow-based backlog refinement process. In the Rock Crusher, big rocks are split into smaller rocks. This is one of several refinement processes. Some of these smaller rocks are valuable and right-sized and the team pulls them through the thin pipe. Other rocks represent valueless overburden and are discarded through the waste gate. But just tumbling rocks through a Rock Crusher is insufficient. At times the team may need significant help refining the rocks to determine which parts are valuable and which parts should be discarded.

Once again, we turn to the mining industry for inspiration. The mining industry uses ball mills to refine mineral-bearing rocks. These large rotating drums are filled with heavy steel balls that crush larger rocks into finely pulverized ore.

Based on this model and our need for some method to visualize incremental analysis and design, we came up with the *crusher*—a special rock used to refine larger, less well-formed rocks into more right-sized and well-formed rocks.

One could think of the crusher as a sort of meta-rock—a rock for learning about other rocks. The intent of the crusher is to learn the knowledge needed to guide refinement of its parent rock.

A crusher does not result in a solution increment. Rather, the outcome of a crusher is usually learning, expressed as a model or a decision. The team then uses that knowledge to guide subsequent refinement of the parent rock. Crushers help the team learn faster and more economically than they would by implementing a feature slice.

The crusher is still a rock, and it must be well formed and right-sized before the team can pull it through the thin pipe. Here, well formed means the crusher will result in demonstrable knowledge. A crusher focuses and timeboxes analysis and design effort so that the team balances up-front design efforts with emergent design principles. When modeling is a faster way to learn about a system than coding it, the Rock Crusher team can make that work visible and manageable by using a crusher.

Well-Formed Crushers

Like all other rocks, a crusher should be well formed, with an intent, a verifiable model, and a test. The intent of the crusher is learning—either creating or discovering the knowledge the team needs to refine a rock.

A well-formed crusher follows the classic user story format:

Description: What do we need to learn and why do we need it?

Acceptance: How will we know if what we learn is correct or has a chance of working?

Here is an example of well-formed crusher:

Understand Engage Art

Create a use case brief of Engage Art so that we can decide the primary categories of services the gallery will provide to its audience.

Acceptance

Use case brief identifies the main actors and their primary workflows.

Provide a table of contents for a potential guide for curating events.

Reviewed by directors and have their agreement.

Figure 6.1: A well-formed crusher can help the team split a big rock into well-formed and right-sized child rocks

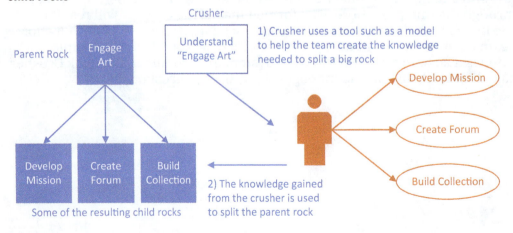

Use Crushers to Make Analysis Visible

The description states the need to create a use case brief for learning the knowledge we need to help us break the initiative-sized parent rock "Engage Art" into its primary service categories. The resulting use case brief is the rock's verifiable model. Further, creating a table of contents for a potential curator's guide based on that use case model will help stakeholders verify the model.

This crusher is fairly small; it's only asking for a use case brief and not a full use case model. If it were too large to complete within an appropriate timebox, the team would have to split it like any other rock that is too large to pull through the thin pipe. In this case, the team can demonstrate the resulting brief and table of content quickly and gain feedback.

Compare the reasonably well-formed crusher to the less well-formed crusher described here:

Understand Engage Art

Analyze Engage Art

This crusher just creates some open-ended work. It has no valuable outcome specified by an intent. There is no way to know what the team wants to learn or when they are done.

Crushers and Spikes

Crushers are analogous to spikes—a common agile term for an exploration story. Teams frequently create spikes when they need to discover an answer to a question, usually for a technical solution.

While a spike is an example of a crusher, we did not want to redefine a commonly used and understood agile term. Most teams use spikes to answer questions about how they will implement the solution—building the thing right. Crushers are more about answering questions about the problem the team is trying to solve—building the right thing.

The technical nature of spikes highlights the code-centric view of the backlog held by many agile teams. The spike is commonly understood as an explicit backlog item the team pulls to learn how to approach coding a solution. It is much less common to use a backlog item to learn about the problem the team is trying to solve or to design the solution.

An important common truth about spikes and crushers is that they require team capacity. That is, because you are doing this thing, something else will have to wait. One description of a spike is "spending team capacity to buy knowledge that you couldn't get any other way." A spike by itself does not create end-user value in the form of delivered code. Similarly, a team placing a crusher into the backlog is elevating the importance of that activity and committing some part of limited team capacity against it. They are buying knowledge—knowledge of what to build versus how to build—because they have decided it is essential to do so.

Highlighting the Value of Modeling

"All models are wrong but some are useful" is a famous saying attributed to George E. P. Box. You may have heard this in other circumstances as "the map is not the territory." Both sentences are ways of saying that a representation of a thing is never the same as the actual thing but there's still a lot of value in having an understandable representation.

During product development a model will often offer the team tremendous value at a relatively low cost, especially when that model is an alternative to creating working software. Using a model can accelerate the agile feedback and learning cycle when it is a valid and productive alternative.

Unfortunately, modeling is often mistakenly considered taboo in the agile community; widespread misuse of modeling has associated it with big up-front design.

Yet, whether we acknowledge it or not, development teams are in the model building business:

- A business has a model for how it operates, and its practices, processes, and workflows are all part of that model. Code can be a machine-executable realization of that model, as can business procedures for manual operations.

- Trains are controlled using either a fixed-block signaling model or a variable-block signaling model. The sophisticated code of automated railway signaling systems is a realization of those models.

- The sophisticated code of flight management systems implements critical mathematical models of flight dynamics.

Regardless of the domain, whether it is clean and mathematically elegant or rules-driven with strange and bizarre edge cases, software implements a model of reality. While working software may be the gold standard for a verifiable model, less formal and less precise representations of verifiable models are also effective for learning.

Well-formed crushers improve the value of modeling by limiting its scope and making the required learning explicit. Like any other rock, a crusher needs an intent: What do we need to learn and to what level of precision? A crusher results in a verifiable model: How will we represent that learning (a use case, a state transition diagram, a customer journey)? How will we test the resulting model to demonstrate that it is correct (a review, a demonstration, a simulation)?

Like all other rocks, crushers need to be right-sized so they do not clog the thin pipe. We want the right level of analysis and information—not too much and not too little.

The Economics of Accuracy and Precision

To make good decisions, we need accurate answers to questions. We do not necessarily need precise answers. For example, say I do not like going skiing if the lift lines are long. To decide whether to go skiing or not, I just need to ask a friend who is already at the mountain whether it's crowded. I do not need to know precisely how many people are on the mountain. Even if my friend knew that number, it is unlikely it would improve my decision-making in any meaningful way.

Agilists have a saying: "I'd rather be roughly right than precisely wrong." We can agree it's crowded. Whether crowded means 400 or 500 people really isn't important because the net information is the same and it is fit for use. If I'm going to ski today, I have to plan on crowds.

Although we may want to believe that more precise learning is better, we must account for how long that learning will take and what it will cost. Most people think of this under the heading of "the point of diminishing returns."

What level of precision do you need to answer the questions the team has about a given rock? If the team is exploring a user interface design, will a simple paper mock-up be sufficient? Can we just get the UX team in a room and get opinions versus getting a full user mock-up done and end users in a research lab? The first is inexpensive and quick, the second requires funding and time.

Greater precision always comes with a cost of greater time and effort. Good engineers and analysts always ask "What is the fastest and cheapest way to learn what we need to learn?"

Levels of Modeling Precision

To facilitate consensus around the level of precision needed in our modeling, we have created a three-level scale.

- **Level 1: Verification by consensus or conversation**. This is a subjective, imprecise verification that results from the review of a document or model. An example of a level 1 verification is walking through a scenario using a whiteboard sketch and getting feedback and acknowledgment. At a minimum there is agreement, and perhaps even a sign-off.

  This is a fast and economical approach to understanding the problem and solution space early on when dealing with very large, ambiguous rocks. Level 1 precision is often associated with answering the question "In general, are we all agreed we may be building the right thing?"

  Typically, level 1 verifications are an economical way to quickly learn paths forward and pave the way for more precise learning opportunities (level 2 and level 3). Level 1 verification could be considered as establishing a hypothesis that the team can validate using a more expensive and precise level 2 or level 3 verification. Invalidating a hypothesis at level 1 is the fastest and cheapest way to avoid building the wrong thing (overproduction).

- **Level 2 Precision—Verification by sample or proof-of-concept**. Level 2 precision introduces objective evidence by generating a proxy data set the team can demonstrate and use to explicitly verify the model. For example, the team may be able to model a system behavior using a state machine and demonstrate that the model forecasts the system will respond correctly to varying inputs in different states. Or the team could create an executable user interface and solicit test subject feedback. The model could also be an early, possibly not production ready release of some part of the system, demonstrating that the system works and could satisfy the intent.

  The key distinction of level 2 precision is that this is more than an opinion. There is testable data, but that data is a proxy indicator for a fully working end product.

- **Level 3 Precision—Verification by final-quality deliverable**. At the level of completed, working software, level 3 is the standard of meeting acceptance criteria, passing quality checks, and similar finalization activities. In terms of rocks, which may or may not be software, this is objective proof that the deliverable meets the Definition of Done.

Validation Examples

The three levels of precision can help the team quickly and incrementally learn and discover what they need to create a valuable solution increment. Let's walk through examples for a moment. For our purposes here, assume the team is building a software application. They are investigating a new feature they think would be valuable, but the feature might be too complex to use easily, which would negate its value.

Rock, Level 1 Validation (Consensus)

Intent: We believe this feature will be a competitive advantage AND we wonder if the design can be resolved to be simple enough to enable it.

Verifiable Model: Email proposing this idea to a key group of stakeholders, asking if they agree it will be a good thing to pursue.

Test: Did they say yes?

Let's say the stakeholders did say yes. The team marks the crusher completed and makes a new one, which might look like this.

Rock, Level 2 Validation (Prototype or Design)

Intent: We believe that this design, shown in the rock, would be worth testing with a focus group and stands a good chance of passing the ten-second standard we hold for "easy learning."

Verifiable Model: Annotated graphic design created for critique by UX professionals and stakeholders.

Test: Team reviews the design—an objective but not working model—and agrees that it stands a good chance of meeting the need.

The team meets, updates the design slightly in a workshop, and then gives the model a thumbs-up to progress to a focus group.

Rock, Level 2 Validation (Prototype or Design)

Intent: As a user of this application, I want to understand how to use [this basic capability] in under 10 seconds, via simple discovery and without investing time in training.

Verifiable Model: A simple mock-up, in a computer but NOT working software, shown to users in a structured focus group with the question "Please indicate how you would do [this thing]."

Test: Time how long it takes the user to figure out what to do under controlled conditions.

You read that correctly—this is also a level 2 validation. The team isn't building any software yet.

The team can all observe the testing and bring a timer. If the user figures the feature out in less than 10 seconds, everyone knows, objectively, that this design will meet the intent. The team would test a spectrum of users to ensure they get a good sample.

If the design passes the test, the team will write up the necessary rocks to author the software. At some point these will be pulled through the thin pipe. At this point, they will be verifying an end product they have built. In addition to the usual software testing and quality checks, the team will run the 10-second UX test for the end product.

Rock, Level 3 Validation (Working Software)

Intent: As a user of this application, I want to understand how to use [this basic capability] in under 10 seconds, via simple discovery and without investing time in training.

Verifiable Model: Using the working software, we will give new users the task and see how long it takes them to figure it out.

Test: Time how long it takes the user to figure out what to do under controlled conditions.

The design was faithfully built and previously passed the test, so the team naturally expects it to work. But what makes this different from level 2 is that the team is testing actual working software in the real world, where many things can go wrong:

- What if something that wasn't present in the mock-up interferes?
- What if by the time the user gets to this part of the software we have inadvertently taught them that the system works opposite to the way this particular feature works?
- What if the user does something we didn't expect them to do?

A working prototype could never fully replace a real-world test of real-world software. That's the difference between level 2 and level 3.

Level 3 precision is the most expensive form of testing because the team has to build the real thing. With level 1 and level 2 models, the team just refines what they can before moving to construction. Although we always want to learn from the outcomes of actual construction, when there are better, faster, and cheaper ways of gaining that knowledge we should typically use them.

Balancing between appropriate advance learning and ideation and the risk of falling into "analysis paralysis" comes from experience and skill.

This example took you through some of the rocks a team might construct. Consider the depth and breadth of rocks they could have constructed and tested. No team could test all of the verifiable models of all of those rocks. Instead, a team may form many rocks, refine some, and reject many. Ultimately, splitting all of these rocks results in final pulls through the thin pipe into the development team for creation of end-user value.

Managing the Flow

Many organizations professing to manage flow are frequently oblivious to the analysis and design work done by their senior engineers and analysts. These enterprise subject matter experts are the keepers of the enterprise domain and technology, involved in all new enterprise initiatives determining precisely what to build. Yet in most enterprises there is little to no demand management for these experts beyond how many meetings can be scheduled into their day. They usually work at extremely high utilization levels, which is an economic disaster for the enterprise. As a result, they are busy, but not much is getting done.

Senior engineers and analysts are a common bottleneck in most organizations. While we may be able to go out and hire more skilled developers, it often takes years for an individual to learn and understand the domain and systems of an enterprise. If we are to get our best possible economic outcomes, then we need to focus on the flow of all the work, not just the implementation work.

Part of what prevents us from managing all the flow is a culture that assumes analysis and design work is just part of the job for senior engineers and analysts. After all, they should know how to manage their time. But if we honestly believe in Lean and Agile economics, then we need to manage flow rather than utilization. Few senior engineers and analysts have any visibility into their workload beyond what's on their calendar. Very few can tell you how much work in progress they have or their lead time for getting a job done. Without this knowledge we cannot manage flow. We just assume that if someone is busy then they are getting things done.

Enterprises are further discouraged from managing all the flow by assuming that a large initiative is only "in progress" when a development team pulls a well-formed story from their team backlog for implementation. This is a vestige of the backlog as a reservoir mindset. To manage all the flow, we have to consider a rock "in progress" the moment the team needs to involve scarce resources such as senior engineers and analysts. The team can use crushers to visualize and manage their work in progress. The experts can measure their lead times. The organization will be able to manage flow.

Avoiding Stealth BUFD

Crushers are about making the flow of analysis design work visible and therefore managed. They should represent right-sized chunks of learning that facilitate rapid incremental development and exploration of the problem and solution spaces.

But crushers can also be misused and abused. They are not an excuse for traditional big up-front design.

You should immediately question an approach where you see any of the following:

- The backlog consists mostly of crushers.

- After many weeks there is no working software.

- Crushers are typically level 3 models, bypassing the value of level 1 and 2 validation.

The intent of a crusher is to accelerate learning and speed the delivery of working software, not to slow it down and design everything up front.

Decisions about whether to use crushers should be driven by one simple question: "What is the fastest and most economical way to deliver working software that is fit for purpose?"

Use Crushers to Make Analysis Visible

Summary

- A crusher is a rock with an intent of creating the knowledge needed to progressively refine an abstract rock into more concrete children.
- Crushers are an alternative to relying completely on emergent design or big up-front design.
- Crushers are useful when modeling may be the fastest and most economical way to learn.
- A crusher helps make the entire flow of value visible, beyond just the implementation work.

Try This

- How is analysis and design work visualized in your team? Is it considered part of the work for delivering on a classic user story—for example, a typical user story involves some analysis and design, implementation, and testing—or is it just assumed that "someone" will get it done?
- Is analysis and design work considered an up-front activity done outside of the team?
- Are there examples of work products in your organization that represent each of the three levels of precision?
- Talk to some of your senior engineers and analysts who are frequently involved in discoveries and design. How are they tracking all their work in progress? Do they know what their lead time is? Do they have a day job in addition to their "consultative" work?

7 Crushing Rocks the Right Way

Learning Objectives

- List good practices for facilitating the learning process during refinement.
- State the differences between refinement and a classic work breakdown.
- Explain how incremental delivery can quickly validate a model and accelerate learning.
- Describe three general strategies for refining rocks and when to apply them.

Backlog refinement is a learning process. Alistair Cockburn's quip that "a *user story is a promise for a conversation*" highlights backlog refinement as a learning process. A user story often starts off as a vague description written on a sticky note: "I want to withdraw money from my account so I can go buy things." In textbook Agile, the team sits with their product owner and has a conversation to learn the intent and scope of the story. The team asks questions and the product owner's answers usually become the story's acceptance criteria.[1]

In backlog refinement the team uses the knowledge gained through learning activities such as conversation, modeling, and coding to guide decisions and create well-formed, right-sized rocks from poorly formed large rocks. During backlog refinement with the rock crusher, ss a part of that learning, the team discovers the real gems and discards the overburden through the waste gate. They may also discover that the rock's scope is large, and therefore further refine the rock by splitting it into smaller child rocks.

---

1. Portions of this chapter were previously published on steveadolph.com in a variety of articles.

Refinement happens all the time, and covers a wide range of activities and practices. There are generally three approaches to refining a rock:

- Conversations and informal models. Agile is about "individuals and interactions," and a rock's intent and scope are easily learned through conversations and whiteboards.

- Create a crusher. Sometimes, refinement requires field work and serious thinking. The team may need to reach out to subject matter experts, analyze data, or research third-party products. Understanding the problem may require more formal modeling than a sketch on a whiteboard. For these situations, the team can add a crusher to their backlog to visualize and manage this work.

- Just code it. Models are appropriate when they are the fastest and most economically appropriate approach to learning what the team needs to know to refine rocks. However, sometimes it is cheaper and faster to implement a production-quality slice of the solution and learn from that, even at the cost of rework.

Value Breakdown versus Work Breakdown

A common misconception is that the hierarchy created during backlog refinement is analogous to a work breakdown structure (WBS). It's easy to see why; after all, the team can represent the history of refinement as a parent-child hierarchy between rocks. But the likeness is only superficial.

The intent of backlog refinement is to discover the valuable increments of a large rock by breaking it down by value—finding the gems. We can implement that gem and demonstrate a small but valuable slice of the desired outcome. Refining a rock in this way creates a value-based breakdown. This is what enables the incremental delivery of value in agile and therefore enables us to manage value delivery.

In contrast, traditional work breakdown approaches would break a rock down by work activity. This is not a trivial semantic difference—value versus activity. If the team breaks a rock down by activity (work), they are managing cost and timelines, not value. Most traditional work breakdowns do not generate any value until all the work is done. But if the team breaks a rock down by value they can deliver that value incrementally, greatly reducing lead times and increasing learning cycles.

Rock Refinement Techniques

Teams create crushers when learning what they need to know will take significant effort and they want to make that effort visible, but most refinement activity does not involve a crusher. For example, a simple whiteboard conversation between a couple of team members may quickly create the knowledge needed to refine a rock.

Agile methodologies are based on a very simple idea: Get something of value done quickly. This is why most agile frameworks favor short iterations and small user stories or backlog items. The intent is to get things done within an iteration's short timebox and then quickly get feedback from the stakeholders.

The problem is that most work does not originate as nice small rocks that the team can deliver within a single iteration. Rather, most work starts with large or mountain-sized rocks. There is a significant refinement process for breaking those massive rocks down into boulders and eventually into rocks that the team can pull through the thin pipe. Agile fiction and coding-centric thinking makes us believe that an omniscient product owner magically conjures well-formed, right-sized rocks for a team.

In waterfall frameworks, this refinement is done up front. In agile frameworks it is done progressively and empirically. The team thinks a little, codes a little, validates their thinking, learns, and then repeats the cycle. In this section, we present three techniques for refining large, poorly formed rocks into smaller well-formed rocks.

A classic backlog refinement guide is Bill Wake's "Twenty Ways to Split Stories."[1] We have consolidated these 20 ways into three general refinement strategies: model-driven, acceptance criteria-driven, and low-fidelity/high-fidelity.

Figure 7.1: Strategies for splitting epic rocks into smaller rocks

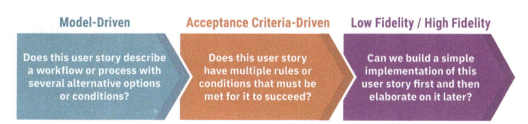

---

1. Wake, B. *Twenty Ways to Split Stories*. XP123. 2005. https://xp123.com/articles/twenty-ways-to-split-stories/.

Model-Driven Refinement

Model-driven refinement is based on the principle that the verifiable model for a rock can be expressed using modeling tools such as customer journeys, use cases, and state transition diagrams. The knowledge created by building those models helps the team discover the small increments of value—the gems—hidden inside.

Many agilists don't see user stories as models, but Jeff Patton's story mapping approach encourages us to view the end-to-end interaction and flow of the user experience as a series of user activities and tasks, with the user stories fitting inside the frame of the map. This is a model, and one which we strongly encourage you to explore.[1]

Use case and scenario models are one way to refine a rock. A use case diagram can quickly guide the team's refinement along the lines of transactions that are valuable to the users. Most well-formed use cases are organized as a "main success" scenario plus a number of alternatives. Each path through the use case or scenario is valuable in some way and can become a child rock. Figure 7.2 shows how a team could apply the use case model to refine a rock called "Upgrade Seat" into three smaller, well-formed child rocks.

1. Patton, J. *User Story Mapping: Discover the Whole Story, Build the Right Product*. O'Reilly Publishing. 2014.

Crushing Rocks the Right Way

Figure 7.2: Splitting rocks using a use case model

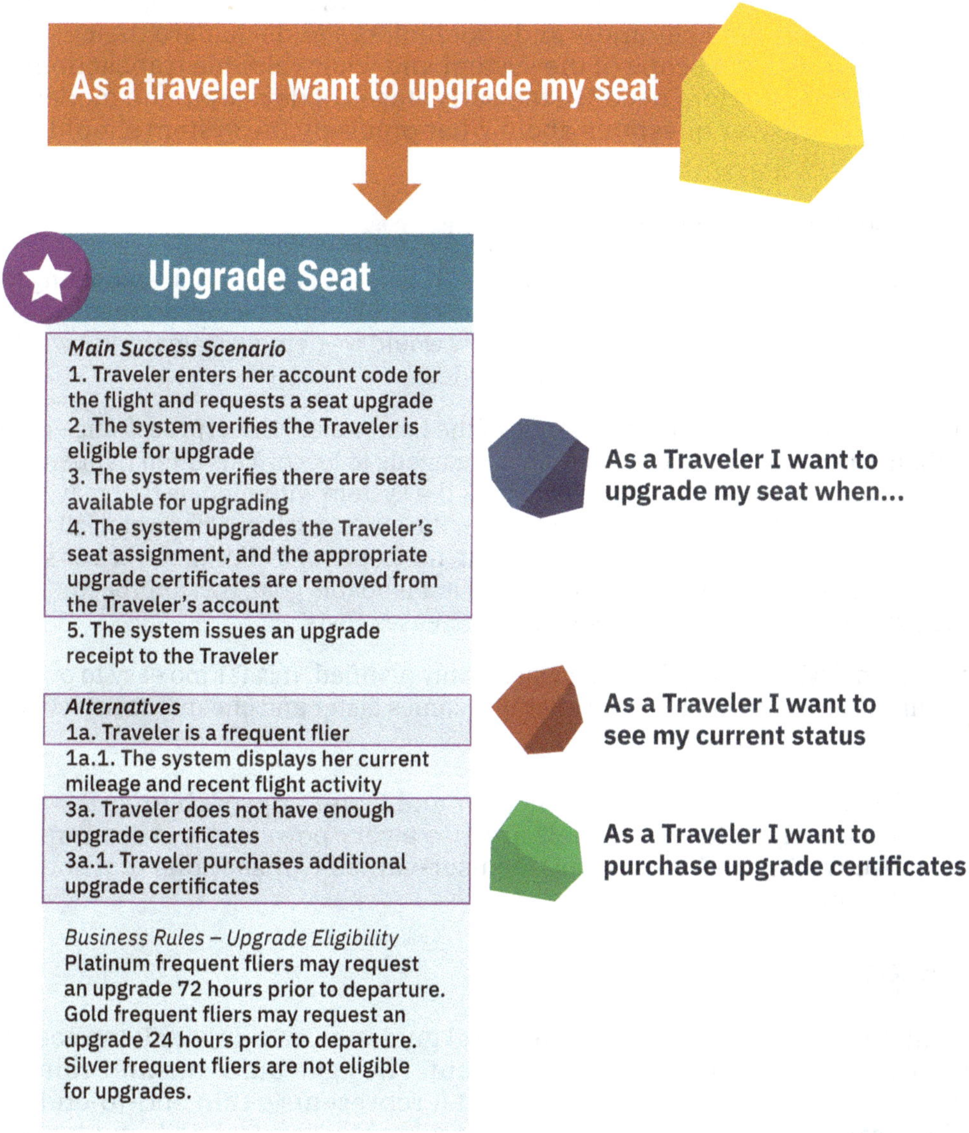

As a traveler I want to upgrade my seat

⭐ Upgrade Seat

Main Success Scenario
1. Traveler enters her account code for the flight and requests a seat upgrade
2. The system verifies the Traveler is eligible for upgrade
3. The system verifies there are seats available for upgrading
4. The system upgrades the Traveler's seat assignment, and the appropriate upgrade certificates are removed from the Traveler's account
5. The system issues an upgrade receipt to the Traveler

Alternatives
1a. Traveler is a frequent flier
1a.1. The system displays her current mileage and recent flight activity
3a. Traveler does not have enough upgrade certificates
3a.1. Traveler purchases additional upgrade certificates

Business Rules – Upgrade Eligibility
Platinum frequent fliers may request an upgrade 72 hours prior to departure. Gold frequent fliers may request an upgrade 24 hours prior to departure. Silver frequent fliers are not eligible for upgrades.

As a Traveler I want to upgrade my seat when...

As a Traveler I want to see my current status

As a Traveler I want to purchase upgrade certificates

Model-driven refinement will likely be more useful earlier, when a team developing a larger system is trying to understand how to refine the mountains. Usually, they will ask questions such as, Who are the customers and stakeholders and what are their customer journeys? What is the scope of the system and what valuable transactions do those customers and stakeholders need? In the early stages of development, models are a cheap and fast way to answer questions about what precisely the system should do and how big it is.

There are three modeling anti-patterns to watch for:

- The model is not validated. Drawing a diagram on a whiteboard is a legitimate modeling tool, but it is not a useful model if the team cannot validate it. Remember, a well-formed rock results in a testable verified model. Always ask, How would we demonstrate the knowledge we gained by building this model at an iteration review?

- The model is overly precise. This is an example of the Lean waste of overprocessing—doing more work than is necessary to learn what the team needs to learn. This often happens because people confuse models built to learn about the system with models that may be needed later to document the system. Furthermore, the stage gates in older waterfall frameworks often required highly precise models in the hopes of avoiding rework or scope creep in subsequent stages. While avoiding rework is a laudable goal, this approach generally delays learning and value delivery and increases costs.

- Continuing to model when it is no longer economically justified. It is far too easy to over model—to continue building models long after it becomes faster and cheaper to just code the system.

Model-driven refinement is probably a far cheaper and faster approach to understanding a rock early in its life. Models are also a very powerful and economical tool early on for discovering and preserving the user-valued transactions that could be lost with other refinement techniques.

Architectural Models

Very few agile methodologies provide architectural guidance, making it all too easy to ignore the use of architectural models in refinement. The agile unicorns-and-rainbows ideal for a backlog item such as a user story is that it represents a thin end-to-end slice of functionality through all the layers of a technology stack. Classical agile guidance is that architecture emerges through incremental delivery and aggressive refactoring of the system. The benefit of this approach is that agile feature teams can pull a story from the backlog and quickly deliver user-facing functionality that does not depend on the completion of another story. This helps us reach the Lean and Agile ideal for delivering a flow of value.

Sometimes this ideal can be achieved, but for large, complex systems or legacy architectures it may not be possible, or even desirable. Knowledge and expertise are not evenly distributed among all developers. There are the engineers who have a deep understanding of the funky quirks of the system's custom operating kernel and core systems. There are those wonderful creatives who understand UX design and create a truly delightful customer experience. There are the math wizards whose minds live in some otherworldly n-space and have an impenetrable understanding of the proprietary algorithms. There are the specialized database engineers. And there are engineers who have a deep understanding of commercial software like SAP or Peopleware.

Architectural models can help inform refinement decisions by helping the team understand rocks from multiple points of view—especially larger rocks. Architectural modeling involves creating multiple models for a rock that clarify its behavior and how that behavior is implemented by the architectural elements of the solution. There are numerous guidelines and recommendations for doing this, including Philippe Kruchten's 4+1 Model[1] and Simon Brown's C4[2] model.

Using multiple points of view to understand a rock may result in child rocks that directly implement user valuable transactions and rocks that will be needed to enhance the solution architecture to support those transactions. The team may need child rocks to implement new algorithms, APIs, and data stores to realize a user valuable transaction. One risk to this approach is that it may lead to artificially refining the rock by architectural elements rather than trying to seek an end-to-end implementation. This is why it's important to see the rock from multiple viewpoints.

Acceptance Criteria-Driven Refinement

Another value-preserving refinement technique is acceptance criteria-driven refinement. A well-formed rock has a list of acceptance criteria—the testable criteria that the backlog owner needs to see met before they can accept the rock. Each set of acceptance criteria represents something of value to a stakeholder, so the resulting children will generally represent a user-valued transaction.

A rock with acceptance criteria is already fairly well elaborated and is likely coming close to being ready for implementation. During a backlog refining session, the team members can estimate the size of the rock to determine whether they can reasonably commit to delivering it during the planned time period. If not, the team may want to refine the backlog item by splitting the rock using the acceptance criteria already

1. Kruchten, P. *The 4+ 1 View Model of Architecture*. IEEE Software 12, no. 6 (1995). 42–50.

2. Brown, S., and Betts, T. *The C4 Model for Software Architecture*. InfoQ, June 25, 2018. https://www.infoq.com/articles/C4-architecture-model/.

defined. Figure 7.3 shows how a large rock—in this case, a large user story—can be refined into smaller rocks that will better flow through the thin pipe.

Figure 7.3: Splitting rocks using acceptance criteria

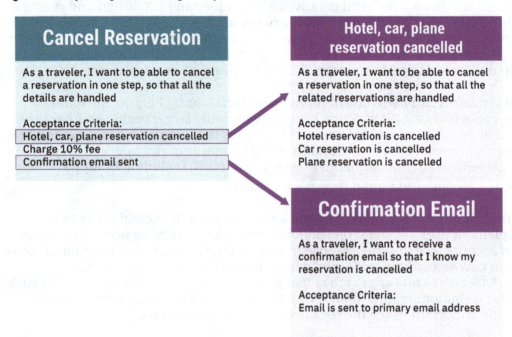

Acceptance criteria can be used to inform decisions on how to refine a rock that is too large to be confidently completed within a reasonable time frame. Each set of acceptance criteria provides a way to progressively grow the delivered product until the team realizes enough of the functionality from the larger rock to ship it.

Acceptance criteria-driven refinement is usually used when a near-ready rock is too large to pull through the thin pipe. The team could apply model-driven refinement, but they may be able to refine the rock faster and cheaper by driving to reasonable acceptance criteria.

Low-Fidelity/High-Fidelity—Incremental Development

This is a more traditional method for refining rocks. The team starts by creating a low-fidelity implementation of the rock, to make sure it works, and then incrementally creates higher and higher fidelity versions as they refine the functionality. A classic example of this approach is deferring implementation of a sophisticated user interface.

The team can develop a simple form-based user interface—or even just an API, depending on the type of system they are building—and then add selection boxes, widgets, icons, and other tools and decorations later. Incremental development also works well when the value or risk is associated with implementing an algorithm—the team can start with the simplest thing that will let them prove that it works, and add more complexity and sophistication to the design later.

Figure 7.4: Splitting rocks using low-fidelity/high-fidelity implementations (incremental development)

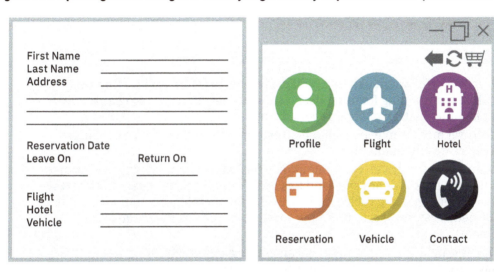

Many developers are reluctant to take a low-fidelity/high-fidelity approach because it implies rework. For example, building a low-fidelity user interface that is later followed by a high-fidelity user interface seems to be redoing UI development work. But we must consider the rework cost within a total economic model: The team is incurring a transaction cost by doing the UI twice, but they will reduce overall lead time, increase throughput, and deliver a product that is better fit for its purpose than they could create otherwise. This hesitancy is often more common where there is a high transaction cost associated with the practices in the thin pipe, perhaps because completing a story requires many manual steps—manual reviews, manual testing, manual integration, etc.

This is a more engineering-driven approach to refinement than other techniques. The essence of lo-fi/hi-fi is to defer engineering refinement until the team has evidence that they are moving in a functionally valuable direction. Some describe this approach as first creating a skeleton that can walk. Once the walking skeleton is validated, they begin to flesh it out. This is a superb way to avoid overengineering a system, or to validate an architectural model early. Far too many systems that looked great on paper delivered subpar performance when implemented, if they could even be implemented.

In summary, low-fidelity/high-fidelity refinement is useful when a rock is still too big to pull through the thin pipe after applying model-driven and acceptance criteria-driven techniques. This helps avoid the waste of overprocessing in the form of gold plating (building in features and functionality that nobody needs), and avoids the waste of overproduction by reducing the risk of building the wrong thing right. The team gets fast feedback from the low-fidelity implementation of a feature before investing effort in creating a high-fidelity version.

Summary

- Model-driven refinement can be a cheap, fast way to refine wishful thinking rocks while maintaining focus on user-valued transactions—as long as the team doesn't fall into the trap of big up-front design.
- Architectural models may be useful to provide multiple viewpoints of a large rock and create alignment around technical work.
- Acceptance criteria-driven refinement may be faster than modeling, and is most useful when a rock is near ready and has well-formed acceptance criteria. While this is useful for splitting rocks, it's less useful for overall refinement (because well-formed acceptance criteria imply a well-formed rock that needs little refinement).
- Low-fidelity/high-fidelity refinement can create a demonstrable system quickly, but may obscure the user-valued transaction if used too soon. Lo-fi/hi-fi is probably inappropriate if there is a lot of manual effort involved in rework.
- Teams should be careful to split rocks by value, not by technology layer.

Try This

- What role does your team play in backlog refinement?
- Does most backlog refinement occur inside or outside of your team?
- Does your team actively collaborate with the product owner and other stakeholders to determine the intent and scope of rocks, or is most of your backlog refinement just right-sizing rocks?
- What activities does your team perform for backlog refinement?
- Do you have regular backlog refinement meetings?
- What other activities does your team do to contribute to backlog refinement (learning about rocks)?
- Can you find examples of the three refinement techniques in your organization?
- What is one Rock Crusher practice you might try to improve your backlog refinement process?

8   Backlog Refinement with the Rock Crusher

Learning Objectives

- Explain why the backlog refinement meetings are important for maintaining flow.
- List four questions that can be used to prioritize rocks.
- Produce an ideal agenda for a Rock Crusher refinement meeting.
- Explain the difference between cost and value and why cost is not a good proxy for value.
- Explain how to use the cost of delay to determine the economic value of a rock.

The backlog refinement meeting is a regular team meeting where the team collaboratively refines rocks to help maintain flow and decide precisely what to build. It is where the team and the village collaborate to inform the backlog owner about the decisions that must be made to stabilize and throttle the turbulent flow through the Rock Crusher. Newly arrived, poorly formed rocks may displace well-refined rocks. Previously ready rocks may be deprioritized in favor of new ones.

During the backlog refinement meetings, the village collaborates with the backlog owner to make the hard economic decisions which agility demands.

Working together, the village will complete several activities:

- Intake new rocks and create a shared awareness of those rocks.

- Align the team to backlog content and create awareness of upcoming rocks.

- Ensure the team is not starved for ready rocks.

- Ensure the right rocks are moving through the Rock Crusher in a timely manner.

- Decide what refinement must be accomplished to get a rock from its current state to ready.

- Eject "debris" through the waste gate—that is, remove rocks from the backlog that are not considered valuable.

By evaluating rocks "upward" through the Rock Crusher—from rocks that are ready or near ready to those that are wishful thinking—the team effectively pulls rocks through instead of pushing them.

Figure 8.1: Working up through the Rock Crusher to pull rocks through

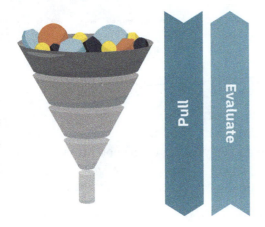

Avoiding Planning Panic

The first question many agile coaches will ask a team that is having problems planning and delivering work is "Do you have a regular backlog refinement meeting?" The lack of a regular and effective backlog refinement meeting is the root cause of many problems that keep a team from reliably delivering on their commitments. A common "bad smell" of a poor backlog refinement process is planning panic—the realization, in the middle of a planning meeting, that the highest-priority rocks are not ready. Planning panic can become a planning crisis when the team cannot even size a high-priority rock because they have no real idea of the scope.

Teams need domain and technical knowledge to refine rocks which may be beyond the team's collective knowledge, and they may need to consult a subject matter expert outside of the team. Unfortunately, the needed outside subject matter experts are rarely available on short notice. Often, teams in the grip of a planning crisis will just go through the motions of committing to the rock and hope that somehow a miracle will happen. Teams caught in this cycle often experience hangovers—rocks that cannot be completed in a timebox and hang over into the next one, or even the timeboxes after that.

These issues are avoided with a regular backlog refinement meeting. During a backlog refinement meeting the backlog owner presents a rock for the team to consider, and the team learns about the rock by asking questions. If they need to consult outside subject matter experts they have time to go find those experts and ask for advice. If the team has technical implementation questions, the refinement meeting gives them time to perhaps add a crusher to the backlog. They have plenty of time to learn what's required to make a rock ready, in plenty of time to avoid planning panic.

The Backlog Refinement Meeting

The backlog refinement meeting is a regularly scheduled event running from one to two hours. Any given meeting might focus on a different planning horizon of work, tactical or strategic.

A team-level tactical backlog refinement meeting should generally occur at least once a week, while more distant-looking strategic backlog refinement meetings may be scheduled every two to four weeks.

Agenda

Regardless of the planning horizon, backlog refinement meetings use the follow agenda:

- The backlog owner welcomes team members and others.

- The backlog owner reviews the solution objective, setting the focus and reminding everyone of the organization's current priority.

- The backlog owner and team review changes to the backlog since the last meeting, including new rocks that have been added to the funnel.

- The backlog owner might "walk up" through the rocks in the Rock Crusher's funnel, from ready and near-ready rocks through the forecasted, speculative, and finally wishful thinking horizons. This fast walkthrough helps the team align on the current context and prepares them for the more detailed discussion around readiness.

- Starting with ready rocks, the backlog owner walks back from the highest priority to lower-priority rocks, determining their readiness.

Determining the real readiness of each "ready" rock takes most of the time in this meeting. For each ready rock, the team and backlog owner will collaborate on several activities:

- The backlog owner presents a rock that is not ready for pulling through the thin pipe, and the team asks clarifying questions about the rock. During the process, the backlog owner expresses the value of the rock. Value may be determined informally by expert opinion or through a value model.[1]

- The team collectively sizes the rock using some form of collaborative sizing technique, such as planning poker or a sizing board.

- The backlog owner considers the value and size of the rock and decides whether the rock is still worth it. If it is not, the rock might be ejected through the waste gate.

- The team and backlog owner review the rock's readiness and, based on the value and size of the rock, determine the next steps to get the rock "ready."

- The backlog owner may eject the rock through the waste gate because it has expired. A decision rule sometimes helps here; for example, "A user story rock expires if it has not been touched or worked on for (say, one or two months)," or "An initiative-sized rock expires if it has not been worked on for (say, three or four months)." This keeps zombie rocks from clogging the Rock Crusher; otherwise, the team might easily waste time justifying why a particular rock is being kept around.

- If the rock satisfies the team's Definition of Ready, such as "ready to pull," it is set accordingly in whatever tool the team is using.

- If the rock is close to final readiness, the team may do the remaining refinement work to get the rock to ready during the meeting.

- If the rock requires extensive investigation to decide how to appropriately refine it the team may investigate further via a spike (to investigate a technical question of critical importance) or by scheduling a crusher.

- After discussions with the team, the backlog owner may decide that the rock is no longer worthwhile and eject it through the waste gate.

- For each rock the team considers and does not eject through the waste gate, the backlog owner may reprioritize the rock based on what has been learned during the meeting. Although the backlog owner is accountable for the priority of rocks, it is helpful to have the team's input in making prioritization decisions.

---

1. Choo, J. *The Value Model: The Missing Ingredient that Makes All the Difference in the Strategy Journey*. 2017. https://www.linkedin.com/pulse/value-model-missing-ingredient-makes-all-difference-strategy-choo/.

The Four Refinement Questions

Effective backlog refinement means asking four questions about each rock the team considers during a backlog refinement meeting:

- How valuable is this rock? The backlog owner is accountable for prioritizing rocks in the backlog to deliver the best value to the organization, so the backlog owner needs to know the value a rock could add to the solution. Some backlog owners are also solution owners who intuitively know the value of a rock through their intimate understanding of the marketplace. Others may collaborate with a solution owner, other stakeholders, and the team to determine the objective, defensible value of a rock.

- How big is this rock? The team cannot plan if they do not know how big the rock is. A rock may contribute significant value, but if that value requires significant effort then it may not be worth it. In addition, a team needs to know how big a near-ready rock is to decide whether they can pull it through the thin pipe without clogging it. Oversized rocks may need to be split into smaller chunks that can flow through the thin pipe.

- Is this rock worth it? After the team knows the value and size of a rock the backlog owner needs to determine whether the rock is still worth it. A rock with huge potential value for the organization may also require a huge investment of time and effort. The fundamental assumption of the Rock Crusher is that organizations have limited resources and cannot pursue every idea. Pursuing one idea means forgoing another; pursuing a large, valuable rock could mean passing on a set of smaller rocks that collectively deliver more value sooner. This is why the Rock Crusher has a waste gate.

- How ready is this rock? If the backlog owner decides the rock is still worth it, then the rock can be appropriately prioritized. This is when the team determines what they have to do to get this rock ready. Is minor refinement during the backlog refinement meeting enough, or is more investigation required? The team may need to create a crusher to refine the rock.

Optimizing Refinement

Like any good Lean system, the Rock Crusher is a pull-based system. As the team pulls ready rocks, additional rocks are made ready so that the team is never starved for rocks. A reasonable guideline is to have up to two iterations worth of ready rocks.

It is important not to over refine or have an excessive supply of ready rocks. Too much refinement just creates wasteful work in progress that clogs the Rock Crusher and is the slippery slope to old-fashioned big up-front design. Remember: We are trying to avoid treating the backlog as a reservoir. Simply put, there is little value in refining rocks faster than they can be consumed. Avoiding waste in this part of the process is just as important as avoiding waste for the development team.

The volume of rocks we should consider refining is driven by two factors: the volume of rocks the team can pull through the thin pipe and the average volume of rocks ejected through the waste gate.

The Waste Gate

Figure 8.2: Flow and the waste gate

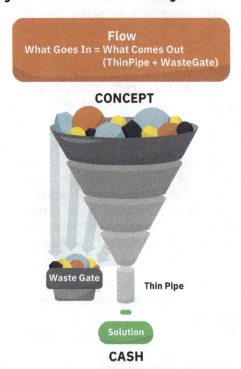

An important activity for stabilizing and throttling the flow during the refinement meeting is deciding which rocks should be discarded. The goal is to avoid the stacked plates model and maintain flow without creating a giant reservoir of ready rocks. To accomplish this, the team must eject rocks that are stale, or which are just tumbling, tumbling, tumbling to no benefit. Both cases reflect a "flow load" that has no value beyond a certain point, and indicate rocks that should be discarded—ejected through the waste gate.

The team may discard a rock early—for example, when they realize an initiative-sized rock will not create any worthwhile value—or later, when they realize a story-sized rock is no longer worth pursuing.

Rocks may be ejected actively or passively:

- *Active* – The backlog owner decides to remove the rock because it is irrelevant or obsolete.

- *Passive* – The rock has aged out; that is, it has been in the backlog so long that it is clear it will probably never be implemented.

It's up to the team to decide how to eject rocks through the waste gate. They may simply delete the rock and forget about it forever. Or they may use something like a "soft delete"—marking an item as "Removed" or "Declined" so it no longer shows as in consideration but could be retrieved.

Attendance

In Agile, "those who do the work, size the work," so whoever is doing the work needs to be in the refinement meeting, or at least represented in the meeting. If a development team is pulling ready rocks into an iteration, then the whole development team needs to participate in the backlog refinement meeting.

Classic agile methodologies usually specify the meeting attendees as the product owner and the team. The Rock Crusher is similar, but we include the whole village: the team, the backlog owner, and maybe the solution owner, analyst, and subject matter expert. Some meetings may include the stakeholder and even the customer. The attendees should include everyone who is held accountable for decisions and everyone who has the knowledge needed to make those decisions. Typically, the backlog owner, the solution owner, the stakeholder, and the customer know the value of the rock; the team knows how much it costs to implement.

Answering the Four Questions

The participants in the backlog refinement meeting are collaborating to answer the four refinement questions. Here we provide some guidance on how they can do that.

How Valuable Is This Rock?

One frequently cited quote from Donald Reinertsen's Principles of Product Development Flow is "If you quantify just one thing, quantify the cost of delay."[1] In simple terms, cost of delay is the value lost by delaying a rock. This is critical information for the backlog owner because prioritization means delaying one rock in

---

1. Reinertsen, D. *The Principles of Product Development Flow: Second Generation Lean Product Development*. Celeritas Publishing. 2009.

favor of another. This gives the team a structure to evaluate and quantify trade-offs in our prioritization decisions.

Determining the value of a rock is notoriously difficult because, like beauty, value is in the eye of the beholder. Fortunately for backlog refinement, the team does not need a precise quantifiable answer to the question "how valuable is this rock?" You do not have to build a precise financial model and compare discounted cash flows. All you need is a defensible consensual explanation for why we consider one rock to be more valuable than another. Therefore, just as teams use relative estimating to size rocks, they can use relative estimating, intuition, expert knowledge, or a value model to forecast the value of a rock.

How Big Is This Rock?

As with value, you do not need a precise size for a rock. You just need a defensible consensus on the relative size of one rock compared to another. You are only seeking data to inform a decision about which rock should be prioritized ahead of another. This is why T-shirt sizing is a common technique, as is use of the so-called modified Fibonacci sequence (1, 2, 3, 5, 8, 13, 20, 40 ...) or powers of 2 (1, 2, 4, 8, 16 ...). The size question can be answered using collaborative techniques such as planning poker or a sizing board.

Thoughts from Ryland

A best practice is that "the people who will do the work estimate the work." While this may seem obvious, there are environments where "external experts" who are not on the team will estimate what they think it should take. The next time this happens to you—or you happen to be one of the people giving those external estimates—I hope you'll try this thought experiment.

Picture a two-car garage full of junk. Stuff is piled at least six feet high throughout the space. Some of it is boxed, some is scattered around loose. A few of the boxes are leaking fluids. Others smell terrible. Someone you have never met and who does not know your skill set, your physical abilities, what tools you have, and how much time you can commit will decide how long it should take you to clean out this garage.

How would you like to receive that assignment? How accurate do you think their estimate is likely to be? How committed are you going to be to honoring this estimate?

That's the problem with having someone who is not on the team do the estimate. This situation should be avoided at all costs.

Sometimes, the team cannot estimate a rock because they have unanswered questions about the rock's intent. If it's easy to get those answers without disrupting the flow of the estimation session, then you may certainly do so. If it would take too long, then consider creating a crusher with the intent of discovering the data needed to accurately size the rock.

Is This Rock Worth It?

What sometimes gets lost under the radar with the adoption of agile frameworks and practices is that Agile is a value management system and not a cost management system. Costs are not managed because a fixed-size team executing in fixed-length timeboxes predictably fixes the cost.

Value is variable, though, so to manage value the team should focus on always pulling the highest-priority rocks through the thin pipe. In other words, maximize the economic value delivered by investing that fixed team development capacity in the highest value rocks.

When determining whether a rock is worth it, the best economic guidance is to pick the low-hanging fruit. That is, give priority to the work that gives us the best value for the least work—the most bang for the buck. An effective way to quantify this sage advice is using Weighted Shortest Job First (WSJF) to inform prioritization decisions. In its simplest form, WSJF is just value divided by duration.

While Reinertsen's formula uses duration as the denominator, we can use rock size as an easy proxy for time.

$$WSJF = V \div S$$

For the best economic outcome, rocks with higher WSJF scores should be prioritized ahead of those with lower scores. Once again, you do not need a high level of precision to inform decision-making, you just need enough to get a consensus among the village members that one rock should be prioritized over another.

The backlog owner can use the rock's WSJF score to inform their prioritization decisions. If the backlog owner decides the rock is worth it, then the rock remains in the Rock Crusher for further refinement. If the backlog owner decides the rock is not worth it, they can either eject the rock through the waste gate or create a crusher to investigate what is truly valuable in the rock—the pearl in the oyster. The team can often draw on the Pareto Principle to find the 20% of the rock that yields 80% of the value.

A third course of action is to simply defer the rock and hope that something will change to make it a better bet. Avoid this kind of nondecision; it just clutters and clogs the Rock Crusher with zombie rocks. This is also why we strongly recommend "aging" rocks—it forces zombie rocks out through the waste gate.

An even worse prioritization technique is the so-called HiPPO approach, where the Highest Paid Person in the room insists on their preferred prioritization regardless of the WSJF score. Once again, no framework or model can prevent arbitrariness, malice, or capriciousness. It can only make it visible.

How Ready Is This Rock?

If the backlog owner decides the rock is worth it, then knowing rock "readiness" informs the team what level of effort is required to prepare the rock so that it can be pulled through the thin pipe.

- A rock could be well formed and the team can readily size it and have a high degree of confidence in their size estimate.

- A rock could also be a "proto user story" with a poorly formed description and no acceptance criteria. It may take extensive research, analysis, and synthesis to get the rock well formed and ready.

Strategic and Tactical Refinement Meetings

Some stakeholders may not be interested in the technical details that often must be discussed during a backlog refinement meeting. Some may simply not want to have a recurring weekly meeting on the calendar. In these situations, it may be appropriate to introduce a strategic backlog refinement meeting.

A strategic backlog refinement meeting will focus more on ensuring that the rocks the team is refining are aligned with enterprise strategy than their readiness. This is not an excuse for engineering teams to disengage from understanding enterprise strategy, context, and customers; it is simply an opportunity to ensure all individuals in the village, and their efforts, are aligned at a strategic level.

Figure 8.3: Strategic versus tactical refinement meetings

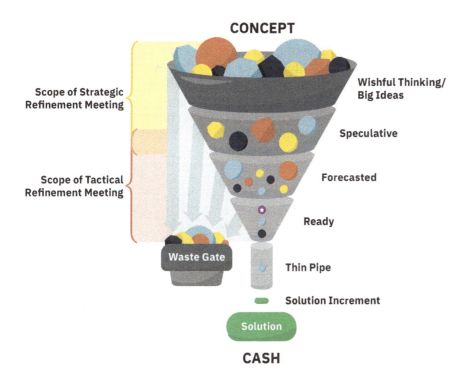

In this meeting model, the traditional backlog refinement meeting would be more tactical in nature, biased toward answering the questions "How ready is this rock?" and "How big is this rock?" In the higher-level strategic meeting, the stakeholders and other key Rock Crusher roles would come together to answer the questions "How valuable is this rock?" and "Is this rock worth it?"

Typically, a strategic backlog refinement meeting will occur at about half the cadence of the tactical meeting. For example, if tactical meetings occur every two weeks, as suggested earlier in this chapter, the strategic meeting may be held about every four weeks.

Typically, one or two senior technical team members should attend a strategic refinement meeting, since they are most likely to know which efforts are easy or hard, large or small. Likewise, tactical backlog meetings should include customer representatives. Although the tactical meetings are focused on readying rocks to pull through the thin pipe, customer representatives and business SMEs will often have valuable input on which rocks are still worthwhile.

Summary

- The goal of the backlog refinement meeting is making the decisions necessary to stabilize and throttle the flow through the backlog. This ensures the team has an adequate supply of ready rocks and that the right rocks are ready.
- A team-level backlog refinement meeting should be held weekly. A team running a two-week iteration often alternates between a regular planning meeting in week one and a backlog refinement meeting in week two.
- The backlog refinement meeting answers four refinement questions about each rock:
  - How valuable is this rock?
  - How big is this rock?
  - Is this rock worth it?
  - How ready is this rock?
- Backlog refinement does not require precise answers to the four questions. Rather it just requires defensibly accurate answers that help inform the backlog owner that one rock should be prioritized ahead of another.
- To explicitly maintain alignment with organizational strategy, it may be useful to have both strategic (enterprise-focused) and tactical (execution-focused) backlog refinement meetings.

Try This

- How often do you hold a backlog refinement meeting? Do you have a standing backlog refinement on the team calendar?
- How many levels of backlog refinement do you have? Who attends those meetings and what are the outcomes?
- Does your team ask any of the four refinement questions during your backlog refinement meetings?
- What determines the value of a rock? Is value determined by the HiPPO (Highest Paid Person in the rOom)? Using expert judgment? By estimating cost of delay?
- How are rocks prioritized (by value, by HiPPO, or some other way)? Do you use both value and size to decide whether a rock is worth it?
- Do you regularly discard rocks from your backlog? Do you have a way to discard rocks?

9 Handling Rocks on and off the Roadmap

"Could you make this small change for me please?"

These are some of the most dangerous words in project or product management, because these "small changes" are almost never tracked or accounted for in capacity planning. When teams accept unplanned rocks without appropriate checks and balances, the organization assumes the following risks:

- Disruption to planned rocks, possibly even important priorities, causing missed sprint commitments or release objectives.

- Rushed quality assurance, allowing defects to slip through.

- Insufficient impact analysis, leading to downstream or "cascade" issues in other parts of the software or organization.

- Insufficient benefit analysis, resulting in waste and/or strategy failures.

Generally, it is best practice to separate rocks for new development from rocks for on-demand operational support. Yet, sadly, best practice is not necessarily common practice. In reality, teams often face requests for transactional, on-demand rocks, typically for operational support:

- User inquiries and help desk requests
- Defect fixes (when these are not planned in the backlog)
- Executive requests and escalations by authorities other than the backlog owner
- Research questions about live capabilities
- Research questions regarding software operation

These unplanned rocks can easily overload the team. At larger scales these unplanned rocks can impact entire releases across individual products or product suites.

Unplanned rocks generally have two attributes:

- They are typically transactional work, meaning the rocks are relatively small and would fit in the backlog as a story or task.
- They are often invisible—what we call "dark work."

Dark work in agile projects is much like dark matter in physics: It's invisible but it has a strong influence on its surroundings. When the team fulfills these ad hoc requests, their expertise is utilized off the books, unaccountably, and the organization loses the ability to accurately manage team capacity and flow. Teams loaded down with dark work are often blamed for not getting things done and missing sprint commitments.

Most agile frameworks assume the team's maximum capacity is 100%, completely independent of the type of work used to fill that capacity—planned, transactional, or dark. In this model, the team is expected to account for 100% of their capacity at sprint planning. The more dark work a team has, the more their velocity will appear to decline. Teams can keep dark work from siphoning their capacity by accounting for every rock they pull.

A significant source of dark work is the consultative analysis and design work senior team members, engineers, analysts, and domain experts often perform for upcoming initiatives and features. It's just an expected part of their job, and it's assumed they should have the maturity and experience to manage it alongside their regular team duties. No problem, right? Probably not.

This is arguably part of their job, but often the only visibility into a senior team member's design work is their meeting calendar. As a result, the senior team members who are instrumental to driving the team's success are massively overloaded. Worse, the organization does not have the data to show this overload, outside of complaints about being overworked.

Crushers are intended to mitigate this problem by making such analysis and design work visible. This empowers senior team members to say "No, I'm at capacity," and shifts the team toward effectively managing capacity and maximizing flow.

Handling Non-Roadmapped Rocks

Non-roadmapped rocks should be managed and tracked in the backlog like any other rock. The backlog is always the single source of work for a team.

Additionally, the backlog owner must still approve non-roadmapped rocks. Remember that the backlog owner is accountable for how they spend the team's capacity. Although the backlog owner may delegate this accountability so the team can manage on-demand and crisis rocks, the person delegated to is using borrowed authority—ownership remains with the backlog owner. For example, in a severity one outage, where a critical system is completely unavailable to users, the team can reasonably borrow authority in the absence of the backlog owner. No reasonable backlog owner would choose to do feature development while a critical business function is at a standstill.

On the other hand, if someone asked the team to change a given background color from green to blue, the team should not accept that work independently. It would be reasonable to wait until the backlog owner is available.

Ideally, though, if the team is genuinely expected to be a product development team, we must work to minimize non-roadmapped rocks.

Managing Incoming Rocks

To start, let's establish some terms so we can more easily picture the types of rocks coming into the team.

- *Planned* rocks appear on the roadmap because they were discovered during the planning cycles. These rocks are typically present in the sprint backlog of the current iteration.

- *Unplanned* rocks are not on the roadmap. No one anticipated that this rock was going to arise during a specific sprint.

- *Expected* rocks are any rocks the team saw coming. Expected rocks may be either planned or unplanned.

- *Unexpected* rocks are any rocks the team had no way of predicting would occur during the sprint.

Combining these terms, we can create a matrix to classify rocks a team may encounter.

	Planned (known)	Unplanned (unknown)
Expected (high probability)	This refers to classic roadmapped Rock Crusher work.	Based on historical patterns, the team regularly receives these rocks and they are managed using capacity allocation. This rock is not on the roadmap, but the team anticipates it.
Unexpected (low probability)	Although the team does not expect this rock, there is some (low) chance it will be needed. The team will have a plan for it, just in case. This is the domain of risk mitigation.	This is typically a crisis or black swan event. The team's only recourse for dealing with this rock is to break the thin pipe, abandon their commitment, deal with the event, and then retrospect to understand what happened.

Planned and Expected: Roadmap or Sprint Plan Rocks

Planned and expected rocks represent classic sprint cycle rocks and are in the Rock Crusher sweet spot. These are the rocks on the team's roadmap. The team generally has good visibility into the current state of these rocks and knows when they will be pulled through the thin pipe. The team can plan rock refinement for these. For a team focused on new feature development, planned and expected rocks should generally account for 70% or more of the team's capacity.

Unplanned and Expected: Capacity Allocation

"Unplanned and expected" sounds like an oxymoron, but it is not. These are rocks the team knows from experience will arise—they just don't know when. Here are some examples:

- Configuring a new user

- Performing technical maintenance

- Requests from high-value stakeholders (in cases where such requests are typical and necessary)

- Allocation of a technology team's time to assist a technical subject matter expert or analyst

Typically, the team cannot decline these rocks due to business impact. Declinable rocks would fall into the planned category and would be allocated to a sprint.

Unplanned and expected rocks should be managed through capacity allocation—holding back a percentage of the team's capacity during sprint backlog planning. This avoids overcommitting the team. In a product development group, this allocation will generally be less than 25% of the team's sprint capacity.

When an issue arises that falls within the scope of the team's reserved capacity, the team creates a rock, refines it, and sizes it as they would for any other work. For example: "Create and configure new user accounts" or "Reserved for SME consultations." Note that this portion of the team's capacity may be limited to specific individuals. For example, a specific senior developer or lead may have 50% of their time allocated to SME/analyst activities, shielding the other team members from interruption (an example of the Sacrifice One Person pattern[1]). Such protection for team members is a core principle in most frameworks because it maximizes overall team velocity.

If the number and size of unplanned, expected rocks are much lower than the team's capacity allocation, the team can pull another rock from the next sprint into the current sprint and start on it early. Another alternative is to keep a list of small technical debt items team members could work on instead.

If the unplanned and expected rocks are substantially larger than the allocation, then the team should consult the backlog owner about whether to honor the unplanned rock or defer it. Sometimes, a delay is not possible. For example, deferring new user accounts to a system for two weeks would likely cause problems for new hires, with all kinds of associated real and perceived problems. In such cases, the backlog owner will have to determine which of the other incomplete rocks in the current sprint can be postponed in favor of the unplanned rocks. Anyone expecting those postponed rocks would likely have to be informed. This situation is never pleasant, and deciding whether the rocks are genuinely not deferrable can be challenging.

Both under- and overallocation scenarios are disruptive and represent a waste of team capacity. If the team allocates too much capacity to unplanned but expected rocks, they may miss an opportunity to deliver value. If they allocate too little capacity, they are certain to miss expected business value because they will have to siphon capacity from planned rocks.

---

1. Coplien, J., and Harrison, N. *Organizational Patterns of Agile Software Development*. Pearson Prentice Hall. 2005.

Planned and Unexpected: Risk Mitigation

Planned and unexpected rocks are not scheduled via the backlog and can arise anytime. These are rocks that may arise at some point, although it is impossible to predict exactly when or even if they will. Predicting these rocks is challenging because they have a very low probability of occurring.

Examples of planned and unexpected rocks include a new software release, a patch, an external system delivering a new interface, or an organizational change that causes mass changes to hierarchy or data. Historically, these kinds of activities have presented no challenges to the team, so there is no reason to expect that things will go wrong in this iteration. However, problems are not impossible, so the team accepts the risk and plans for the unexpected using risk management and risk mitigation plans. Then, if the unexpected does happen, the team knows what to do and how to recover the release.

Unplanned and Unexpected: Retrospective

Unplanned and unexpected rocks occur when the team is confronted with something new which they could not have reasonably predicted.

In these cases, some or all planned rocks must be abandoned in favor of what is likely a crisis. Examples include a server failure, a complete system outage, a crucial partner integration experiencing a system or communication failure, or a significant client requirement that needs attention to avoid a substantial financial impact on the organization.

In a situation like this, all the team can do is work together and collaborate with the backlog owner on deciding priorities. Later, the team should perform a retrospective of the situation. This retrospective is not minor or ceremonial; it should be targeted and is intended to drive a root cause analysis. The goal of the retrospective should be finding ways to avoid the situation in the future or creating a way to move the situation to the "planned and unexpected" category, with a mitigation plan available.

Frequent unplanned and unexpected rocks indicate a systematic issue and require serious attention from management.

Thoughts from Ryland

I once had an engagement doing agile assessment and some coaching with several teams in a company. One of these teams became a good example of a team benefiting from the practices we are outlining here. No dark work was done, and all work was approved by the backlog owner.

Before I got involved, the team was considered a product development team operating at a very low velocity. Management was frustrated: The team was obviously busy but it wasn't creating new products at any reliable or fast pace.

I examined the team's workflow, sat in on sprint planning and capacity allocation, and followed the work as it occurred during the sprint and made several interesting observations:

- The team did typically calculate their capacity successfully at the beginning of each sprint.
- The team did typically successfully estimate the size of user stories.
- The team typically had a lot of hangovers: user stories that were carried from sprint to sprint. Even a small story which should have taken 2–3 days would enter "in progress" status and then stop and inexplicably remain open for as many as 3–5 sprints.
- The backlog had many stories listed as "in progress" that had been halted in favor of other work and never restarted. It was difficult to determine which item was really "in progress" at any time.
- The team was constantly interrupted with work they could not decline—typically, things that would affect revenue or active retail operations. Understandably, this work always took priority.
- Unplanned items were not factored into the capacity plan and were not logged after the fact. Effectively, this became dark work that was not incorporated into future planning.

About half of the team's time was spent on operational problems: the interrupt-driven revenue and operations impacts that could not be declined. This fits our definition of unplanned but expected rocks. The team also dealt with the occasional crisis—typically, researching a possible defect. This happened in approximately 50% of the sprints, and when it occurred it demanded about 25% of the team's capacity. This work could also not be declined, and about half of the time there was no defect and the system was "functioning as designed." The function was correct, but was surprising to the person asking for the research.

Anywhere from 50% to 75% of the actual team capacity was spent on non-feature work. At best, they could spend 25%–50% of their time on new feature development.

Usually, for reasons beyond the scope of this discussion, the actual figure was less than 25%.

In summary, this team was acting in a product support mode and not as a feature development team.

I used my data and analysis to make this clear to the relevant management and leadership. Leadership acknowledged the interruptions and agreed that they were legitimate and correctly routed to the team. They went on to agree that, given the business impact, these items would always take priority over the new feature development work.

Leadership was left to decide whether to make additional staff available so the team could split into separate development and support groups. The support team would need enough people to handle routine issues, since none of the work was deferrable or discretionary. Meanwhile, the designated development team would work on a normal and predictable cadence to drive the product forward.

Leadership's other option was to acknowledge but not change the situation. This would allow the team to accept new features when possible. They would be unable to commit to delivery dates on anything beyond a small size, but they would be supported correctly and everyone would share the correct expectations about what the team could accomplish.

Summary

- Rocks may enter the team's backlog in one of four ways, best described as a matrix of planned versus unplanned and expected versus unexpected.
- All work should be visualized as rocks in the backlog and accounted for in terms of team capacity.
- Dark work is like dark matter: invisible rocks that clog flow and reduce the team's velocity.
- Unplanned rocks typically still need to be approved by the backlog owner, because the backlog owner is accountable for how they spend the team's capacity.

Try This

- List the work items your team has spent effort on in the last two to four sprints, whether they were completed or not. Then ask your team to identify any dark work in those sprints and estimate how much time they spent on each item. Create a matrix and classify each item in these two lists as either planned or unplanned and expected or unexpected.
- How many items fall into each quadrant? (Remember that a product development team should spend at least 75% of all effort on features and capabilities.)
- What percentage of time or work items is dark work? How is this affecting your team?
- What are the sources of your dark work, and what can you do to make this work visible?
- How does your team handle each of the quadrants of the matrix? Does their strategy match the recommendations in this chapter?
- What processes do you have for handling unplanned work?
- Does your team consult the backlog owner about unplanned work?
- Do you have clear guidelines about when the team can accept unplanned work without consulting the backlog owner?
- When did your team last hold a focused retrospective on unplanned and unexpected work, including a root cause analysis?
- Did the team create a contingency plan for such events in the future?
- Has that work reoccurred since that retrospective? If so, did the contingency plan get used?

Handling Rocks on and off the Roadmap

10 Rock Entry through Front and Back Doors

Learning Objectives

- Explain how rocks enter the Rock Crusher flow.
- Identify the possible paths rocks can take getting in and out of the Rock Crusher.
- Describe circumstances that allow rocks to enter the Rock Crusher through the back door, bypassing normal controls.
- Explain how the Rock Crusher works over different time horizons.

Rocks enter the Rock Crusher at different readiness horizons and in different states of readiness. This is a reality of agile projects, and the Rock Crusher accommodates this reality.

In the Rock Crusher, intake is the point at which the backlog owner and team become aware of a rock—a proposed initiative, a defect, a change request, or a piece of work that will enhance the value of the solution. Depending on its perceived value, the backlog owner may dump the rock out through the waste gate without further thought or decide to accept the rock. Accepting the rock means deciding where in the Rock Crusher to place the rock, based on its readiness and priority. Once accepted into the Rock Crusher, the village can begin pulling the rock through until it is either pulled through the thin pipe or dumped out the waste gate.

Intake

All rocks enter the Rock Crusher through the top. Until a backlog refinement meeting or a team stand-up, the team does not know how ready a new rock is and therefore cannot place it in a horizon. New rocks are in a temporary holding state when they enter the funnel, until the next backlog refinement meeting or stand-up.

For teams primarily working from a roadmap, it's probably adequate to review the funnel at regularly scheduled backlog refinement meetings. Teams that need to be more responsive can do these reviews regularly as part of their daily stand-up.

Figure 10.1: A Rock Crusher kanban board with a funnel

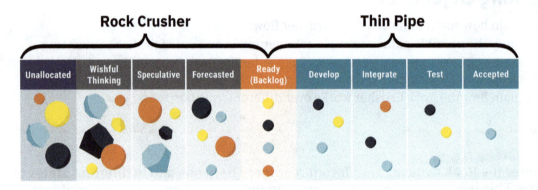

All rocks enter through the funnel—even 911-style hair-on-fire expedited requests. If need be, the team drops everything else they are doing and mobs to determine the size of the request and then begins executing it. Intake can be implemented as an additional state on a kanban board.

The Rock Crusher has two intake processes. The front door is the generally agreed-upon practice for intake, with the backlog owner directly involved in the decision-making process. The front door provides transparency and gives the backlog owner an opportunity to exercise economic judgment and make prioritization decisions. Most rocks should enter here. It represents the official intake rules.

The back door is often an expedited path that bypasses the backlog owner and a lot of organizational processing, such as when a stakeholder directly approaches their favorite team member with a rock. The back door represents the "rules" for breaking the intake rules.

As undesirable as it is, there is always a back door. True, this is bad practice: It consumes capacity that isn't properly managed and lets down the organization. But as a client once said, "What the executive leadership team wants, the executive leadership team gets." Rather than ignoring the back door or pretending we could stamp it out, we chose to acknowledge its existence. Making it visible at least provides evidence of the damage to flow it can cause, and at times the back door is useful for maintaining good relationships with team patrons.

The Front Door

The front door is the primary intake process for most teams, and the backlog refinement meeting is the main intake for the Rock Crusher. During scheduled backlog refinement meetings, the backlog owner and the team evaluate new rocks that have arrived at the funnel since the last meeting.

The backlog's superpower is providing all rocks for a team. Random ad hoc requests and multiple work repositories are like kryptonite to this superpower, introducing significant coordination delays and impeding the benefits of the backlog. Therefore, all rocks—and we mean *all* rocks—enter the Rock Crusher through the intake at the top and are evaluated by the team during the backlog refinement meeting. This way, team members clearly know where their work comes from and what their priorities are. If everyone plays by the same rules all team members will share the same priorities.

During the backlog refinement meeting, the backlog owner presents the new rocks to the team, followed by a discussion about each rock to determine its value, size, and readiness. Based on the outcome of these conversations, the backlog owner can either discard the rock or accept it and place it in any of the four Rock Crusher horizons: wishful thinking, speculative, forecasted, or ready. Most teams hold a weekly backlog refinement meeting, and this cadence should be satisfactory for most work presented to the team. (See Chapter 8 Backlog Refinement with the Rock Crusher for more detailed guidance on holding backlog refinement meetings.)

A weekly intake process may not be responsive enough for teams responsible for work related to operations and running the business. No one wants to wait a week for what they see as a simple configuration request. Many teams use the daily stand-up to evaluate rocks that have arrived since the last stand-up. Teams doing real-time bidding work usually reserve capacity for expected but unplanned rocks and then triage the rocks during the regular daily stand-up. (For more information, see Chapter 9 Handling Rocks on and off the Roadmap.)

The Back Door

There may be situations when the intake process is not sufficiently responsive or seen as an impediment to a simple request. There may be several well-intended requests which come from sources who simply do not want to go through a formal intake process and have the influence to bypass the front door. Before the Rock Crusher, some of these would have been the proverbial shoulder taps, the "could you just do this one quick thing for me please?" requests—a manager going directly to their favorite programmer to make a small change, such as a correction or update to a web page.

Unmanaged, these requests can lead to coordination conflicts, cause wasteful multitasking, and destroy predictability, resulting in lower economic value. Team members could simply learn to say no, but there is also economic value in maintaining good relationships with patrons and stakeholders. Helping them out with small perceived favors will go a long way toward creating a healthy collaborative relationship.

The other common source of back door requests is impatience. If stakeholders believe the intake process keeps them from getting things done, they will just ignore and circumvent it. As Alistair Cockburn once remarked, people trump process. In all situations, there are the rules, and then there are the rules for breaking the rules.

Whatever the motivation, the Rock Crusher's back door makes these requests visible. Back door requests usually are not triaged or deferred, since they generally originate from someone with positional authority or influence. By making back door requests visible, the team can demonstrate how these "simple requests" disrupt the flow, collect metrics on their frequency, and allocate capacity for completing them.

It is important for the team to have strong working agreements for accepting backdoor rocks. Some team members may be too eager to please or may just have a hard time saying no. Strong working agreements will help team members know when they can accept backdoor rocks and when they have to say no. During team retrospectives, the team should review how many backdoor rocks they accepted and the impact of accepting those rocks: Did it make stakeholders and customers happy? Did it damage flow? Does the team need to adjust working agreements?

Thoughts from Ryland

Here is a little story about how to get those working agreements fixed and working with your team and your customer.

I find that programmers, especially the consultants I work with, want to be helpful. This, combined with the difficulty that the younger members of our team had with the idea of turning down a client request, meant that as much as one-third of the team's capacity disappeared into thin air during some sprints. Usually we could account for it after the fact, but the damage was done.

This really was throwing off the team's ability to get things done predictably and with the overall commitments our team had made. I got together with the project manager, Dennis, and we sat down with the team. First, we gently told them that they had to stop doing this. They were giving away their own capacity and this wasn't OK. The sprint work was laid out by us with the product owner, and if they disrupted the backlog we could have a real problem. Second, we gave team members the following script to use if the client—a very hands-on technologist turned IT director—asked them to do work or walk them through a large chunk of code.

"Dave, I would love to (do that thing, or spend time with you), I just have team commitments to honor and I'm on a deadline. Can you talk to either Ryland or Dennis? They can slot this work into the next sprint, or if there is room they can see if we can squeeze it in sooner."

Then we told the client that this was our instruction to the team. We could show him how sprint commitments were being thrown off due his backdoor requests. We let him know that if there were an emergency reprioritization, we would always try to accommodate that—we can break a sprint if we need to!—but this wouldn't help make progress toward the release goal that the team, including him, was focused on.

These two conversations almost completely stopped the disruptions. We did swap a story out during a sprint here or there; however, it wasn't anything I'd call seriously disruptive, and the team always had a say about whether the swap was OK or not in terms of capacity.

We got back to very predictable sprints of capacity and delivery, and the customer remained satisfied.

In consulting, I'll call that a win!

Rolling Wave Planning with Rock Crusher Horizons

The Rock Crusher stabilizes and throttles the flow of rocks and makes that process visible. In an agile organization (not one that's agile in name only), rocks are always entering the funnel, resulting in a turbulent flow. The Rock Crusher horizons explicitly assume a progressive transition from a high degree of turbulence to a much more stable and well-controlled flow.

Working across multiple horizons enables us to look at the flow of rocks at different levels of granularity, zooming out to see the big picture of work waiting to be done and zooming in to refine close-in rocks in detail when needed.

The agile approach to planning across longer timeframes is to create plans within plans, often referred to as rolling wave planning or multi-horizon planning. Longer-term plans present the shorter iteration timeboxes as a roadmap, and the roadmaps break down into iterations which serve as regular validation of the roadmap and show progress toward the overall organization goals. Iteration planning is still part of each iteration, as are all the other iteration ceremonies, stand-ups, reviews, and retrospectives.

Figure 10.2: A long horizon (or release) timebox with a roadmap of iterations

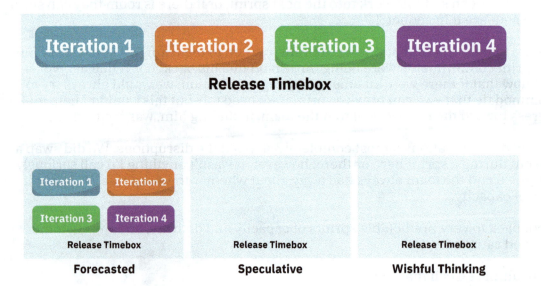

Rock Entry through Front and Back Doors

The Rock Crusher uses four suggested horizons to describe the progressive refinement of rocks in the funnel:

- *Wishful Thinking.* Flow is turbulent: the ideas likely change frequently and are only moderately defined. It is not even certain if a wishful thinking idea will pass vetting. These rocks are difficult at best to prioritize and more or less clustered to some time in the future. Wishful Thinking may represent rocks that should be ready far off in the future, perhaps in two or three quarters or more.

- *Speculative.* Flow at this horizon is less turbulent but with only moderate certainty that all or part of a rock's intent will be needed or will get done (e.g., moderate to large epic user stories). Rocks can be loosely prioritized in clusters. The speculative horizon may represent rocks that should be ready within the next quarter or so.

- *Forecasted.* Flow at this point is significantly smoother. Rocks are near ready, with a good degree of certainty that the team will commit to pulling them through the Rock Crusher, and are either force ranked or nearly so. The forecasted horizon represents rocks that should be ready within a month to a quarter.

- *Ready.* Flow is smooth at this point, and ready backlog rocks are force ranked. The team should be able to pull ready rocks through the thin pipe within the next couple of iterations.

Readiness is loosely correlated to time; that is, the further out in the future the team is looking, the less ready the rock usually is. This avoids the common agile anti-pattern of an overly precise, detailed specification for an initiative or feature that is nowhere near its planned implementation on the roadmap. In addition, higher-priority rocks should be more refined than lower-priority rocks.

Rocks in the wishful thinking and speculative horizons will probably not be sufficiently refined to accurately determine their value or size, making it difficult for the team to force rank or to properly prioritize them. Trying to force rank rocks in these horizons is false precision—a detailed lie that might appease a senior stakeholder but doesn't provide any value to the work. Once rocks are pulled into the forecasted and ready horizons, the team should have enough information to more precisely determine the value of each rock and begin force ranking them to pull through the thin pipe.

There are roadmap-breaking situations where a large, urgent, vague rock is dumped into the funnel. Dropping a rock of this nature into the Rock Crusher is wishful thinking at best. Every team has horror stories about high-priority wishful thinking demands. It becomes near impossible to properly prioritize a rock when you do not know its real value and size and cannot compare it to forecasted and ready rocks.

Sometimes the team can push back against this. Many such requests are not true emergencies. Crises and opportunities will arise all the time; however, the point of agile is to be responsive, not random. Randomness breaks flow.

These are situations that truly test backlog owners. If a wishful thinking or speculative rock is truly time critical, then the first task is to determine the value and size of the rock. This way, the backlog owner can understand the economic trade-off involved in breaking the flow and reprioritizing potentially committed work. Is the economic value of the new opportunity or the risk mitigation greater than the value of the rocks in the pipeline right now?

Summary

- Rocks can enter the Rock Crusher through either the front door or the back door. The front door—the official intake rules—is the preferred entry point because accepting backdoor rocks can break flow.
- In the interest of maintaining good relationships with stakeholders and patrons, it may be necessary to acknowledge a backdoor intake process.
- The team's Rock Crusher will have a back door whether it is acknowledged or not.
- The Rock Crusher explicitly supports planning at different levels of granularity across multiple time horizons.
- During a backlog refinement meeting or a regular stand-up, the team should evaluate newly accepted rocks and place them on the appropriate readiness horizon—wishful thinking, speculative, forecasted, or ready.

Try This

- How effective are your backlog refinement sessions when considering which rocks should be at different horizons?
- Describe and document your team's back door—the rules for breaking the intake rules. What is the process to bring something in through the back door? Who is empowered to do so?
- Identify the work in your current backlog and assign it to the four horizons. How closely does the level of readiness relate to the horizons?

11 Using The Rock Crusher to Facilitate Agile Business Analysis

Learning Objectives

- Define agile business analysis and explain its economic advantage.
- Explain why agility is important to business analysis in rapidly changing complex environments.
- Explain how the Rock Crusher supports the IIBA's seven principles of agile business analysis.

IIBA defines business analysis as "the practice of enabling change in an enterprise by defining needs and recommending solutions that deliver value to stakeholders."[1] This straightforward definition hides the complexity and subtlety of this role, which is supported by a wealth of practices, tools, and techniques designed for different product and project contexts.

Figure 11.1 shows the core concepts of business analysis as depicted in the IIBA Business Analysis Core Concept Model™ (BACCM™).

---

1. International Institute of Business Analysis (IIBA). *A Guide to the Business Analysis Body of Knowledge® (BABOK® Guide)*, v. 3. 2015. 12.

Figure 11.1: The Business Analysis Core Concept Model™

The model has six elements:

- *Change* – a controlled transformation of an organization
- *Context* – the part of the environment which encompasses the change
- *Need* – a problem, opportunity or constraint which motivates a stakeholder to act
- *Stakeholder* – a group or individual with a relationship to the change or the solution
- *Value* – how much something motivates or rewards a stakeholder in a context
- *Solution* – a specific way to satisfy a need in a context

Each of these elements interacts with the others in a constantly evolving learning cycle.

Agile Business Analysis

Agility is embracing change; that is, gaining an economic advantage by learning faster than the rate of change. Agile business analysis is business analysis that enables change in the enterprise that is as fast as or faster than the rate of change in the surrounding economic landscape. It does not take much to imagine what may happen to teams or whole enterprises that fall behind the rate of change. Just ask Kodak, Research in Motion, Nokia, Yahoo, and Blockbuster, to name a few defunct or near-defunct marquee brands, about what happens when you fall behind the rate of change.

According to IIBA:

> Agile business analysis is the practice of business analysis in an agile context with an agile mindset. Agile business analysis can provide a competitive advantage in fast-paced and complex environments and has moved beyond software development initiatives to any business domain. Organizations have adopted agile practices at all levels of planning and in many diverse business areas. A key element of the agile mindset is inspecting and adapting. Feedback at one horizon influences decisions at all the horizons which results in changes to work at the horizons.[1]

Agile business analysis does not change the IIBA Core Concept Model or the knowledge and tools of business analysis. Rather it provides new opportunities to apply knowledge and tools to respond to quickly changing business contexts. Business analysis practitioners use agile business analysis techniques to

- maximize business value,

- rapidly learn, adapt, and respond to change,

- reduce waste by maximizing the amount of work not done,

- acknowledge and manage uncertainty, and

- create a flow of small and valuable components, enabling learning.

Analysts who practice agile business analysis learn what is really needed and valued for a solution before the situation changes. We do not want to be solving last year's problem! The faster the team travels through its learning cycles, the more responsive they are to changing conditions, and the more responsive the enterprise is to its customers.

---

1. International Institute of Business Analysis and Agile Alliance. *Agile Extension to the BABOK® Guide*, v. 2. International Institute of Business Analysis. 2018.

Analysts who flow the backlog using the Rock Crusher instead of using the backlog as a requirements reservoir enable a more agile and responsive enterprise. The Rock Crusher provides a framework and a disciplined approach to identifying changes and bringing them to an enterprise. The Rock Crusher shows the flow of work through the entire value stream, from concept to cash. Business analysts who apply their practices in a traditional big up-front fashion revert to the broken value stream and its economic consequences. They lose the benefits of agility. As we have argued numerous times, Agile is for the whole business—not just the coding team!

Agile business analysis emphasizes the role of the analyst as a co-creator and stakeholder partner—a view that has been sacrificed in some environments where the analyst is sometimes more of an order taker. The Rock Crusher explicitly integrates business analysis activities as part of the value stream and makes those activities visible and accountable, no longer hidden behind the product owner. The Rock Crusher also emphasizes the role of the analyst as a boundary spanner and collaborator; for example, as a thought-partner to the product owner.

Finally, analysts who use the Rock Crusher are better situated to exploit the "build-measure-learn" cycle in strong collaboration with their stakeholders. This helps the team to discover more accurate needs, changes, and solutions, creating overall value more rapidly.

The Value Hypothesis

The agile business analysis fast learning cycle starts with a value hypothesis:

If we do <this> we will realize <this value/benefit>.

This format is tremendously powerful. Analysts must always reside in the idea that they are asserting and testing hypotheses about the problem they are trying to understand. This highlights the value the team hopes to gain by delivering an asset that satisfies the hypothesized need. By using a scientific, evidence-based approach, the analyst makes it clear they intend to *learn* what is valuable to stakeholders.

This approach creates knowledge rather than just opinions.

In following this approach and in collaboration with the team and stakeholders, the analyst will:

- Make observations (e.g., talk to stakeholders about their needs).
- Formulate a hypothesis (e.g., "If we build this then it will satisfy the stakeholders' need").

- Define the leading indicators to test to determine whether the experiment succeeded (e.g., what metrics or acceptance criteria to satisfy, who needs to say "Yes! That's what I need!").

- Conduct the experiment (e.g., build and deliver a part of the system).

- Evaluate the results of the experiment (e.g., demonstrate the system to the stakeholders).

- Determine whether the original hypothesis has been confirmed or rejected (e.g., based on stakeholder feedback, is this solution increment desirable, feasible, and sustainable?).

- Adapt based on the learning, and if necessary, pivot to new topics. Create a new hypothesis using what was just learned.

We can readily see an example of this hypothesis-like format in the user story format popularized by Mike Cohn[1]:

As a <persona>, I want <something>, so that <why>.

The "so that" expresses the benefit hypothesis—what benefit we hope to gain from implementing this user story. When the team presents the deliverable from this user story, a stakeholder (product owner, customer, end user, anyone who is the subject of the user story at hand) can look at it and say one of two things:

- "Yes, that is exactly what I need," which confirms the hypothesis.

- "Where did you ever get the idea that's what we needed?" which obviously rejects the hypothesis.

In either case, the team has learned something valuable quickly, and can then adapt and do the next thing, whether that thing is to continue along the same path or change direction.

Another hypothesis-benefit format suggested by Barry O'Reilly clearly calls out the data analysts collect to validate the outcome:

We believe <this capability>

Will result in <this outcome>

We will have confidence to proceed when <we see a measurable signal>[2]

1. Cohn, M. *User stories applied: For agile software development.* Addison-Wesley Professional. 2004.

2. O'Reilly, B. *How to Implement Hypothesis-Driven Development.* 2013. https://barryoreilly.com/explore/blog/how-to-implement-hypothesis-driven-development/.

A Rock Crusher rock encourages this benefit hypothesis format through the verifiable model described in Chapter 5 Correctly Defining and Managing Rocks.

Figure 11.2: A well-formed rock enables hypothesis testing

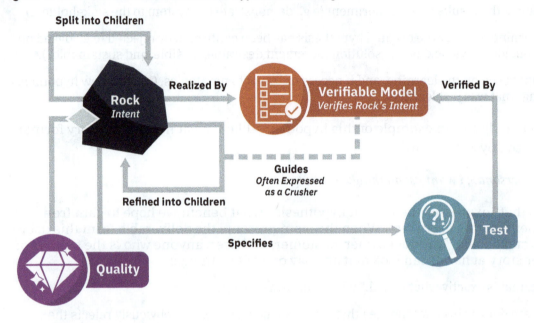

- A rock's intent is ideally expressed as a benefit hypothesis, using either of the formats we shared earlier in this chapter (As-an I-want so-that or Believe–Result In–Confidence).

- The verifiable model is the experiment resulting in a testable asset to satisfy the intent.

- The test is the evaluation of the verifiable model to determine whether to accept or reject the benefit hypothesis.

No matter how big the rock is—initiative-sized, feature-sized, epic-sized, story-sized—or whether the rock is user facing or technology based, we should be able to always express it as "if we do <this> we will realize <this benefit>."

Principles of Agile Business Analysis

The *Agile Extension to the BABOK® Guide* identifies seven principles that guide agile business analysis:

- See the whole.

- Think as a customer.

- Analyze to determine what is valuable

- Get real using examples.

- Understand what is doable.

- Stimulate collaboration and continuous improvement.

- Avoid waste.[1]

These principles are incorporated throughout the Rock Crusher, and are discussed here in more detail.

See the Whole

The Rock Crusher is expressly designed to help the team clearly see the big picture and understand the context in which change is happening. This helps to ensure the right set of needs are met through the solution. The analyst can trace a line of sight from the small rocks in the thin pipe to the medium and large rocks at different horizons, providing a consistent view of the whole and the overall business and customer needs to be met. Backlog refinement activities maintain the overall context of the product being built. This enables other team members to align with the "why" of the individual rocks. Because the whole is not hidden or lost behind a product owner, the team is connected to the whole and the team is connected to the whole and can contribute to driving better economic outcomes.

---

1. International Institute of Business Analysis and Agile Alliance. *Agile Extension to the BABOK® Guide*, v. 2. International Institute of Business Analysis. 2018.

Think as a Customer

Agile business analysts must ensure that solutions genuinely work for the customers. What does it matter if we deliver a technical masterpiece on time and on budget if it does not work for the customer? Analysts must understand customer needs at a level far deeper than only the expressed requirements. They must empathize with customers, collaborate with many different stakeholders, learn, and find ways to bring the voice of the customer to the team when expressing needs and exploring solutions. The Rock Crusher helps analysts do this by moving away from a big up-front analysis process to an approach that rapidly tests the hypothesis of what the customer wants.

The analyst and the customer collaboratively co-create the backlog with deep empathy for the customer's viewpoint, needs, and context. The analyst's customer-centric focus ensures that the right rocks go into the Rock Crusher and guides decisions about what is considered valuable (drawn through the thin pipe) or discarded (expelled through the waste gate).

Analyze to Determine What Is Valuable

The work currently being done should be the most valuable piece of work that could be done. Analysts must understand the many aspects of value and ruthlessly prioritize whatever delivers the most value to the customers, users, the organization, and society.

In the Rock Crusher model, the analyst ensures the presence of well-formed rocks that express the intent of the business need. This provides clarity around the value of the solution. The analyst also ensures that the hypothesis and verifiable test contained in each rock are tested in each work cycle. The team then adjusts course based on those tested outcomes.

Get Real Using Examples

Examples help the team derive acceptance criteria and design the solution, and provide a foundation for testing the solution. In the Rock Crusher, the analyst may treat examples as individual rocks, each with their intent and verifiable model. This removes ambiguity, validating that the example illustrates the value to the business and the customer. Verified models can be further refined, explored, and validated constantly in the flow. In the ideal case, the team frequently puts increments of a working solution into the hands of customers, providing iterative opportunities to ask customers and stakeholders if the solution is fit for purpose.

Understand What Is Doable

Constraints form an important part of the team's and organization's context. Analysts must understand the limitations of time, money, technical feasibility, team skills, capacity, and availability, be honest and open about what is genuinely feasible, and challenge unrealistic expectations.

By continuously testing hypotheses, a Rock Crusher analyst provides the team with early and rapid feedback. Some of these hypotheses will be about technical feasibility or time and effort, which may help the team at large understand what choices are on the table to achieve customer value within a given timeframe.

Stimulate Collaboration and Continuous Improvement

Analysis is not about carrying documents between different groups of people. It is about bringing the right people together and facilitating conversations in a spirit of constantly learning, seeking feedback, and allowing the solution to adapt as the needs evolve and emerge. In short, be a bridge, not a ferry.

The analyst ensures the team keeps the Rock Crusher at the center of team activity, not hidden behind a product owner or other role. This causes the team to examine the flow and identify ways to improve their process of execution and collaboration. The analyst also ensures that the learning from each rock is visible to the team. This drives rapid learning and feedback about both product value and team process improvements.

Avoid Waste

 Truly agile teams reduce unnecessary effort at all points in the value chain, and prevent unnecessary effort at all points in the value chain. Any activity must be value-adding. Where it is not, it is important to examine it to see how waste can be reduced or eliminated. Use the waste gate to discard ideas that don't contribute to the overall outcomes and advance product value.

Analysts use the Rock Crusher practices to stabilize and throttle turbulent flow by ensuring the team only keeps those rocks that are truly valuable. The analyst also drives the use of the waste gate for the bulk of items that should be discarded as the team learns. By aggressively discarding waste, the analyst prevents non-value-added refinement of rocks that cannot proceed further down the funnel, reducing the team's cognitive load.

Summary

- Business analysis is a skill set and a set of competencies which facilitates back-log refinement.
- Agile development does not do away with analysis; it makes analysis continuous and progressive.
- Agile business analysis is a mindset and a set of practices for creating better economic outcomes by learning faster than the rate of change.
- Agile business analysis is guided by seven principles that support the mindset analysts need to succeed in complex, dynamic environments.
- Expressing needs as hypotheses with associated tests provides a structure for agile business analysis.

Try This

- Read the *Agile Extension to the BABOK® Guide* and review the principles of agile analysis. How might those principles be more affirmatively applied in your current work?
- Review the Business Analysis Core Concept Model (BACCM™). Apply these concepts to your own immediate work or a recent project. Can you clearly assert the needs, stakeholders, value, contexts, solutions, and changes that would have been relevant for that effort?
- Consider how you can express a user need as a testable hypothesis. How quickly can you get feedback to either reject or accept the hypothesis? Is the feedback cycle timely enough to help you learn what the customer really needs?

12 Doing Business Analysis with the Rock Crusher

Learning Objectives

- Explain how the Rock Crusher aligns with the Agile Manifesto.
- State the value proposition for crushers.
- Describe how crushers are used in the Rock Crusher life cycle.
- List seven anti-patterns you can use to assess whether you are using crushers well.

By codifying the concepts we've discussed in the Rock Crusher model, we intend to

- make the non-coding work visible,

- drive collaboration, transparency, and accountability,

- embrace multi-horizon thinking, and

- apply strong agile values beyond just coding software.

Embracing the Rock Crusher practices will lead to faster flow and throughput, a sustainable pace that avoids burnout, and building the right things. The Rock Crusher helps you do just enough planning to enable effective responses to change, and helps you avoid wasting analysis work on features that won't increase value.

Many people who read the Agile Manifesto skip an important point made at the very end: "while there is value in the items on the right, we value the items on the left more."[1]

Agilists do value the items on the right, just not as highly!

Given that, a powerful learning technique we've observed is inverting the agile values to create important thinking questions:

Value: "Individuals and interactions over processes and tools."

Question: What are *just enough* processes and tools to enable individuals and interactions to be powerful?

Value: "Working software over comprehensive documentation."

Question: What is *just enough* documentation to enable us to build valuable working software?

Value: "Customer collaboration over contract negotiation."

Question: What is *just enough* contract negotiation to enable us to collaborate with the customer strongly and powerfully?

Value: "Responding to change over following a plan."

Question: What is *just enough* planning to enable us to respond well to change?

When you pose this kind of question as an agilist, analyst, or backlog owner you start to move away from left-or-right, one-or-zero thinking. You embrace the idea that the world is filled with shades of gray as well as shades of color.

It will take time for these concepts to mature in your work. Embrace an attitude of experimentation and learning. As you probably recall from your first agile experiences, embracing activities, concepts, and practices will help grow your mindset. Every change goes through stages of learning, resistance, adaptation, and growth, and improvement rarely follows a straight line. As you grow in depth and knowledge, improvement can even be cyclical.

1. Beck, K., et al. *Manifesto for Agile Software Development*. 2001. https://agilemanifesto.org/.

Analysis Planning

Many people routinely assemble a plan in their mind and can work to it, but experience a variety of ... feelings ... when asked to document that plan so others can understand it. Remember that in the Rock Crusher we value making work visible, transparent, collaborative, accountable, and sustainable.

If the plan is only in your mind, none of those things can happen. Nobody can read your mind, so no one can understand what you're going to do or collaborate with you if they don't know your intentions. As Ryland has often said,

> *Agile is a team sport.*
>
> *Everyone is in.*
>
> *Everyone plays.*
>
> *Nobody sits on the bench.*

This may seem obvious, yet if your job involves an analysis function (business analyst, product manager, product analyst, subject matter expert analyzing a particular technology or business domain) that function has probably been invisible to your team members.

Have you heard the following from a project manager (or have you said anything like this)?

- Well, I don't know why it will take you three weeks to get the requirements put together.

- The project plan says you have a week. Make it happen.

- We start development Tuesday, so have something written by then.

- How hard can it be? We just need the requirements. You have a template, right?

If being asked these questions—or answering them—made you consider shaving your hair off or running away to a remote island, this chapter can help solve your problem.

BABOK® Guide defines process areas and activities and has a complete Knowledge Area around Business Analysis Planning and Monitoring. Many people pay little attention to this section when it is actually at least as important as anything else in the guide. Failing to plan your analysis as you would any other work deprives you of all the Rock Crusher's benefits.

Analysis planning requires you to ask and answer the following questions:

- What am I trying to analyze?

- What documents (artifacts, models, catalogs) will I create that will store and represent the knowledge I develop?

- Who will consume those end products, and to what purpose?

- What questions will I have to ask, what information must I develop, to accomplish my work?

- Who must I talk with to obtain, or to validate, this information?

- What context do I operate in, and are there priorities or constraints I must accommodate?

- What is the sequence of my activities, from discussions to documents to approvals?

- What level of effort will this take, and how long will it take to spend that effort?

- Are there any roadblocks in my way?

The list could go on, but this is an acceptable first level of consideration for our purposes.

You already answer those questions when you approach analysis. You probably do it intuitively and start making a list of what you need to do. We now challenge you to do this so that others can use the list with you, buy into it, and lend their support and understanding.

With a little practice, this takes no more than an hour or two for even the largest analysis efforts. Remember that this is not about doing the analysis; this is just planning the analysis. And if you are blocked and cannot answer these questions, you now have a basis for explaining why you are blocked to the relevant people in your world.

When you create and show your analysis plan you will help everyone in the Rock Crusher village better understand your approach. The solution owner, backlog owner, key stakeholders, or other involved stakeholders and subject matter experts will feel more understood and involved. They will understand how you plan to attack their problem, and see that you are representing their interests and understand their situation and priorities. If they don't see that in your plan, they will see that they have an opportunity to correct your impressions. They will see the alignment in expectations about their involvement and the involvement of their team. If they need to clear any roadblocks (mandatory meetings, set review cycle expectations, drive business stakeholder accountability), they will understand what those roadblocks are and the consequences of failing to clear them.

The backlog owner, project manager, and scrum master/iteration manager will understand the sequence of your plan and the activities you intend to accomplish, and because of that will have a greater sense of security, confidence, and understanding that the analysis will progress well. They will better understand the level of effort and your dependencies on others (stakeholder interviews, workshops, reviews). They will be able to support and defend the time necessary to do your job, and to better communicate the trade-offs on risks and quality if they don't give you that time. They can see the risks and issues you might encounter and help head them off, making these visible and trackable at the product management or program level. And they will be able to offer input and help if they need to adjust other areas of product development (deliverables, talent, consumable hours) to align with your analysis work.

Finally, your manager or supervisor will have an increased insight into your work and a better sense of you as a competent, collaborative professional willing to take ownership and be accountable to your word. They will see that you are aligning expectations with your colleagues and will expect a better outcome: fewer emergency escalations and lower crisis risk in the organization. They will appreciate the proactive approach and be better able to support you because of it.

In short, this may be the most valuable couple of hours you ever spend in product development.

Creating Crushers

A key idea of the Rock Crusher is that all the work from all of the team is reflected in a backlog. We can and should isolate the development work explicitly to the development team to help them focus and avoid interruption, and that is reasonable. But for many analysts, the idea that their work will be in a backlog, visible to sprints and possibly asked about often, is a bit unsettling. It may be a new concept, but don't let it disturb you.

The work items you're doing can be represented as crushers in the Rock Crusher. Making these activities visible as rocks shows the team how much work you are doing and how it is progressing. When someone asks "Can't you do it faster?" or "What's taking you so long?" you will be able to refer to the backlog for answers:

- "Could we narrow the scope to something tiny? If so, I could get dev-ready work done in that narrow scope faster, and keep working on other things while the team builds that."

- "Well, my big delay is that this group of stakeholders isn't available. They don't return my calls and have missed two meetings with me. Can someone lend some executive firepower to make our effort a priority for them?"

- "This item—meeting with the manager of the call center—uncovered a lot of impacts to his team. Maybe the technical lead and I can meet and find a way to minimize those impacts, so we can start on something sooner?"

Your work is now visible and transparent. Everyone should understand what it takes and not expect you to make the requirements magically appear. You can show the timeline on which your work occurs and how it is progressing. You can adapt to change because you have used just enough process and just enough planning to enable you, and the team, to be responsive to change. The team can understand why the plan isn't working as you expected and collaborate with you to do something better.

The following table gives some examples of how common analyst artifacts could be positioned in the Rock Crusher as crushers. Each of these could be a rock which results in refined knowledge rather than a solution increment.

Usual analyst artifact	Intention	Verifiable model	Test (Level of Validation[a])
Elicitation notes	Find out what this given stakeholder experiences as a problem and sees as a solution.	Notes from conversation.	Send notes to stakeholder OR show them as taken; ask if everything is correct, any mistakes or changes from what they meant to say. (L1)
Personae	Answer the question, "Who will use our solution? Who are we designing for?"	A list of personae covering our expected needs for the next three months of effort. Includes a descriptive name, some information about who they are and what they know, and what they intend to achieve by using our product.	Review and approval meeting with project sponsor, key stakeholders, and technical lead. (L2)

Usual analyst artifact	Intention	Verifiable model	Test (Level of Validation[a])
Entity relationship diagram (ERD)	What are the entities and objects of interest in our problem, or in our solution?	The entity model, including identified optionality, cardinality, relationships, and primary key identifiers.	Review and approve the ERD with relevant stakeholders. (L2)
Use case scenario	What are the possible situations our personae will find themselves in? What are the normal paths and the likeliest exception paths?	Your use case template of choice, showing actors, expected activity, expected results, and possible exceptions.	Review and approve the document with relevant stakeholders. (L2) [b]
Context diagram	What is our initial belief about stakeholders, capabilities, and systems which may be involved in the solution?	A context diagram showing stakeholders, possibly personae, capabilities, and high-level existing or future state solution components. (This is likely created through a requirements workshop.)	Acceptance of the initial diagram, possibly at the same meeting where it was created. (L2)[c]
Agile Epic	What is a valuable "chunk" of work that we can do, but which is too big by itself to do in one iteration? What will it do, and not do, and what stories might we need about it?	A written epic, with relevant supporting documents and possibly a sketch of what stories might result from it.	Review of the epic with the relevant stakeholders. Useful and implementable technical and business feedback about what stories will result from it. (L2)

Usual analyst artifact	Intention	Verifiable model	Test (Level of Validation[a])
Agile User Stories	What small and valuable increment of software will we actually build at this point? What acceptance criteria should we apply to it?	Working software code which meets the acceptance criteria of each story that was written.	Review of the completed and working software resulting from each user story. Quality assurance or business representatives acknowledge that the software meets the acceptance criteria and quality standards it is expected to meet. (L3)[d]

a. The level of validation achieved by the test (see Chapter 6 Use Crushers to Make Analysis Visible).

b. As written, this example shows some depth to the use cases. You might have a rock which is limited to the happy path. That will be sufficient for many purposes downstream. Later, you may elaborate your document with the unhappy paths, richer exception handling, and so on. They can easily be different rocks; there's no reason to hold back the value of getting the happy paths approved and into use by other team members.

c. As in other items, this artifact might be decomposed into an initial context diagram and a later refinement of it, depending on consensus when it is written.

d. This is the only level 3 validation item in the list. This is because only the verifiable model created by this item meets the standard of being a working solution increment-actual code which does something valuable for the end user and which can be tested as such. The verifiable models of all other items are either conversations (L1) or a "model representing the real world" (L2). The working software, for our purposes, is the "real-world" test situation.

Just Enough Analysis Planning

As with anything else, there is such a thing as too much or too little planning. Agile approaches certainly require a lot of planning, although people are often surprised by this statement. What would happen if you spent no time planning the work for a sprint or omitted all the time stacking and readying a flow of work in a kanban? Obviously, those activities would likely fail.

Similarly, most agilists would reject the idea that you should have four or five sprints worth of team capacity totally ready for coding and delivery and that the prioritization of the backlog must be locked into order for that long. That is the other extreme: far too much planning.

Use just enough of this—not too much or too little. For your own work, with your own team, there is likely a broad zone of OK between those markers.

How do you know you're in the right space? If you can answer yes to all the following criteria, then you're probably doing OK:

- Do these rocks add clarity and understanding among the team members?

- Do these rocks produce valuable conversations and interactions in proportion to the work needed to track and manage them in the backlog?

- Are these rocks useful to people beyond the analyst who has to own them?

- Is the team able to answer questions about increasing speed, overcoming roadblocks, creating value, and eliminating waste by using these rocks?

In short, if you're getting something valuable out of the effort of showing these analysis rocks in the first place, then you're probably doing something right.

Just like anything else, though, crushers can be misused and abused. Here are a few anti-patterns to be wary of. We describe them as "smells" to leverage the same concept from agile process and user story smells, a common learning technique.

Crusher is not right-sized

This smell occurs when the crusher is not completed within a single iteration (or within the appropriate service level agreement for a Kanban team). The intent of the Rock Crusher is to make the work required to learn precisely what to build visible, and to enable the team to effectively manage that work. If the crusher is too large, open-ended, or allowed to roll over from sprint to sprint, then the work is effectively invisible and unmanaged. A team in this position risks sliding back into big up-front design.

Like all good ready rocks, a crusher must be right-sized. That always means it can be finished within the Kanban SLA or a sprint.

Crusher does not include well-defined, testable acceptance criteria for its learning outcome

This smell usually occurs when the crusher specifies what it will deliver, but not the why. Simply saying "create a use case model for backlog item xyz" may not foster learning. We must declare what we need to learn, or what we expect to learn. Sometimes we may not learn what we want to learn, and that is learning in itself.

If you cannot say why you are doing a piece of analysis work and what value you'll get out of the activity (eliminate risk, identify value, etc.), then why are you doing it?

Crusher is "private" to the analyst

This smell occurs when the analyst believes they have personal ownership of the Rock Crusher process and fully directs it. This reduces transparency and alignment. The Rock Crusher is meant to help guide the team in deciding precisely what to build and quickly create alignment. This cannot happen if the analyst treats the resulting models and work as their personal property. The result is an old-fashioned "throw it over the wall" mentality, where the analyst creates user stories and the team simply implements them. This situation can occur in enterprises that are organized as functional silos and explicitly distinguish between "the business" and "technology."

Crushers are tasks

This smell occurs when the analysis work for implementing a rock during an iteration is broken out into functional rocks such as analysis, design, implement, and test. This can easily lead to waterfalling an iteration and creates excessive work in progress.

Just as we do not create separate rocks for coding and for testing, we do not create a separate rock for analysis if it is a normal part of the work the team can do to implement a ready rock in a single iteration. It is not unusual for an analyst to be a development team member who collaborates and swarms with developers and testers to implement a rock and deliver a solution increment.

Crushers are about getting rocks to ready, not about partially implementing ready rocks.

Most of the backlog items are crushers

This smell occurs when crushers are used to implement a stealth big-up-front-design process. While the first iteration or two of a big rock may be highly biased toward a lot of crushers, you should be suspicious if working solution increments do not soon start emerging—especially if most of the crushers are resulting in level 1 verifiable models. This means you have people talking about things and agreeing, but nobody is putting any work into writing or creating software.

Crushers are mandated as part of the development methodology

This smell occurs when the organization's software development process mandates the use of crushers rather than letting the team determine their economic utility. This often results in a lot of busywork creating models when either a spike or simply implementing a part of the system would create validated learning faster. It delays progress, and the resulting crusher is not valuable.

The fidelity of a crusher is mandated

This smell frequently occurs in regulated organizations where traceability is required to demonstrate compliance. Models are often a big part of this traceability. However, there is a significant difference between the purpose of the models created by a crusher and the purpose of the models we require for traceability and compliance.

- The purpose of a crusher is to generate verifiable knowledge quickly and economically for a team. Tracing isn't typically needed here.

- A traceability model is primarily a documentation model that accurately describes the system's intended behavior with a reasonably sufficiently high level of fidelity that auditors can use it to verify the resulting system.

Traceability models are usually part of the Definition of Done. This level of fidelity may be far above and beyond what the team requires to create verifiable learning quickly and economically.

Summary

- Using crushers creates greater transparency, accountability, value, and flow for a team.
- Like any other rock, crushers should have an intent, a verifiable model, and a test that meets one of the three levels of validation.
- By making analysis work visible and transparent, crushers increase collaboration with team members and stakeholders.
- There are seven anti-patterns you can use to judge whether you are using too many or too few crushers in your work.

Try This

- Write your analysis plan and show it to the right stakeholder(s). Get their feedback about how the plan helps them understand your work and timeline better, or not.
- Consider your analysis plan in terms of what stakeholders you will need involved. Are the people you need available rapidly and easily, or slowly and with difficulty? What does this mean for the rate at which you can work to meet your definition of Ready to Develop?
- Identify the analysis artifacts created by your crushers or in your analysis plan. Does each artifact meet the standard of creating new and valuable information? Is the value of the work proportionate to the effort required? Are there any items you should adopt, replace, or drop from your plan?

13 Is It Working? Rock Crusher Metrics

Learning Objectives

- List the three broad categories of Rock Crusher metrics and several different metrics in each category.
- Explain how OKRs (Objectives and Key Results) can support alignment from business outcomes to delivery of individual rocks.
- Explain how to calculate the crush ratio and understand what it says about the turbulence and flow in a value stream.

Appropriately used metrics are a powerful tool for learning how well the value stream performs. They can reveal bottlenecks, measure how much value the team is creating, and show whether improvement efforts made a difference. But when used improperly, metrics are worse than lies, reinforcing our biases and hiding the real problems in our value streams.

Agilists commonly criticize the project management iron triangle for leaving out the most important metric—value delivered. A project that delivers the defined scope on time and on budget without creating any value is not a successful project. Yet many agilists commit the same sin by measuring only hygiene and performance metrics such as velocity and declare themselves good at creating outputs. Success is often expressed as completing stories in less time—higher velocity. This fixation on velocity is often called "output agile." To use an automobile metaphor, our engine may be performing well and our car may be traveling fast, but are we going anywhere useful? Hygiene and performance metrics are necessary, but certainly not sufficient.

Metrics Categories

The appropriate use of metrics means knowing what the metric can measure and understanding its limitations. By combining the appropriate set of metrics, a team can learn a lot about what happens in their system and how it works.

We can group metrics into three categories: outcome, performance, and hygiene.

Outcome metrics determine whether the team's output is creating and delivering meaningful value for the stakeholders (e.g., cost reduction, increased revenue, improved customer engagement, reduced employee turnover, and risk reduction). If metrics are our car's dashboard, outcome metrics are like the GPS, telling us whether we are on track to reach our destination. Outcome metrics ask:

- Are we building the right product?

- Will the end product create the value we intended?

Performance metrics measure output performance—velocity, throughput, cycle time, and so on. Some teams may also use quality metrics such as defect density to measure the quality of their output. These metrics are like a car's speedometer and compass, telling us how fast we are moving and in which direction. Performance metrics tell us how well the system is operating.

- How well our team operating as we build this product?

- How effective is the flow of work across the team?

Hygiene metrics measure how well the team executes processes. They are often discovered using maturity surveys. Sometimes hygiene metrics are a reasonable proxy for performance; for example, a team with poor practices is not likely to have a high velocity. They are like our car's engine instrumentation, tachometer, water temperature, and oil pressure gauges. These inform us of the health of the engine, but are unable to tell us anything directly about the car's speed or direction. Hygiene metrics ask how smoothly the team is creating together:

- How well are the people collaborating—both within the team and across the greater stakeholder community?

- Are the individual team members feeling safe and able to perform at their best?

- Is each component well-built and healthy—are we building the product right?

This concept can be complicated for people new to the idea, so here are a couple of examples.

Metrics

Scenario	Outcome	Performance	Hygiene
A Scrum team making software	• Deployable and valuable software • End-user feedback measures such as customer satisfaction • Reduced end-user task time	• Team velocity • Escaped defects • Solution server demand/load	• Measurements of WIP for Dev, QA, etc. • Team satisfaction • Demand/load by component (database, API, website)
An assembly line making widgets	• Demand for widgets • Sales of widgets • Customer satisfaction regarding widgets	• Number of scrapped widgets per 1,000 produced • Widgets created per hour • Lead time for special order widgets	• Assembly line speed • Defects per line station • Widget materials on hand

Correctly identifying the category of metric you are using is key to understanding what it can tell you—and what it can't tell you. With this understanding, you can construct monitoring and measurement systems to support your team in their goals, and to know when you are being asked to apply or monitor metrics that are inappropriate to your team. With the right metrics, you can better understand the overall value being delivered, the quality of the product being built, the processes being used, and most importantly the health of the people building the product. Long-term outcomes depend on healthy teams working at a sustainable pace in a psychologically safe environment that enables innovation and creativity.

Connecting OKRs and Metrics

Metrics measure the factors important to the enterprise and answer the question: Are development efforts advancing the enterprise strategy? Since about 2018, Objectives and Key Results (OKRs) have become a popular tool for creating alignment and measuring outcomes.

OKRs can consist of metrics from all three categories. Typically, the focus is on the "important" outcome measure, which is related to the O or Objective—for example, increased speed, decreased cost, or higher customer satisfaction. Additional metrics, both hygiene and performance, indicate whether the team is doing the activities expected to create the outcome.

An OKR "helps to ensure a company focuses efforts on the same important issues throughout the organization."[1] The objective expresses the desired goal, and the key results describe how the organization will measure reaching that objective.

One of the superpowers of OKRs is their ability to align an organization to desired goals. We can express enterprise strategy as a set of OKRs. Departments, value streams, and teams can align themselves by expressing their own OKRs that also align with the enterprise OKRs.

The Rock Crusher is part of a value stream, and the team should create OKRs for the value stream that are aligned with the strategic enterprise goals. Measuring these value stream OKRs tells the team whether the value stream is creating the desired outcomes.

Objective: Reduce lead time to create greater stakeholder and customer satisfaction.

Key Results:

Reduce lead time by 30%

Reduce "expedite" requests by 50%

Increase client NPS[2] by 15%

Like any measurement system, OKRs can be, and often are, misused and abused. They are supposedly a collaborative goal-setting system for aligning teams, but many organizations seem to have forgotten the collaborative part and have turned them into the millennial version of management by objectives. But what gets measured gets done.

1. Doerr, J. *Measure What Matters: How Google, Bono, and the Gates Foundation Rock the World with OKRs*. Penguin. 2018.

2. NICE Systems, Inc. *What Is Net Promoter?* 2021. https://www.netpromoter.com/know/.

If the key result is measuring the wrong thing or measuring something that does not make a difference to the objective, the thing being measured will still get done—especially if it is linked to employee compensation. Teams can often avoid this dysfunction by working collaboratively on OKRs.

Performance Metrics

While we should not confuse output metrics for outcomes, we still need to measure outputs to judge the health of the system itself. We need to measure how well our system is performing. Performance metrics are useful for discovering and diagnosing issues in our flow: what comes in; how long rocks remain in the crusher; when and how they go out, through the waste gate or the thin pipe. We recommend two metrics for this purpose: the flow framework and the crush ratio.

Flow Framework

The Rock Crusher is a flow-based model for managing the backlog, so we can use flow metrics to determine how well work flows through the whole value stream. Mik Kersten's Flow Framework[1] provides excellent metrics for understanding the health of the value stream by relating different flow metrics to business results:

- Flow Velocity – The number of flow items completed over a given period. While analogous to the agile concept of velocity (a measure of throughput), flow velocity is less granular since it measures the number of items completed and not the volume (size or story points) of those items.

- Flow Efficiency – The ratio of active time versus wait time out of the total flow time (activity ratio).

- Flow Time – The total time from starting to completing the work, including both active and wait states across the entire value stream (lead time).

- Flow Load – The ratio of flow items (features, defects, risks, and debt) completed over a given period (loosely related to capacity allocation or backlog color).

Flow metrics provide insight into the operating performance of the value stream, like an automobile's speedometer and compass. However, these metrics do not tell us if we are doing the right thing—creating value.

---

1. Kersten, M. Project to Product: How to Survive and Thrive in the Age of Digital Disruption with the Flow Framework. IT Revolution. 2018.

When applying the flow framework to the Rock Crusher, our goal is to connect the descriptive process metrics of the flow framework to the idea that the solution is supposed to create value for the organization.

The flow metrics feed into the outcome metrics and enable us to gauge how well the product is performing against them. If we consider outcome metrics in light of our process metrics, we will find insights between the two. This may in turn help us focus where to spend our efforts on improving our process.

Outcome metrics include elements such as these:

- Value – The benefit to the business produced by the product value stream.

- Quality – The quality of the product produced by the product value stream as perceived by the customer.

- Happiness – The engagement of the staff working on the product value stream.

- Cost – The cost associated with delivering the product to the business.

Flow metrics can provide insight into how well we are on track to achieve the outcome metrics.

- Is flow velocity stable, increasing or decreasing? Stable or increasing flow velocity may indicate increasing value.

- Is flow efficiency optimal—are there lengthy waits due to task switching and changing priorities? How is this impacting happiness in the team?

- Is flow time reasonable for the type of work being undertaken? What would it take to reduce flow time? Does this have an impact on cost or quality?

- Is the flow load steady and sustainable? Can it be improved?

Crush Ratio

The way value streams are presented often implies that the flow is smooth and all work flowing through the value stream gets done. This may be close to the truth in manufacturing, but it certainly should not be the case in solution development. The Rock Crusher assumes that flow is initially turbulent and must be stabilized and throttled. Since what goes in, must come out, we provide two ways out of the Rock Crusher: the thin pipe or the waste gate. These two ways out give rise to a metric we call the *crush ratio*, a measure of how many of the rocks entering the Rock Crusher are ultimately pulled through the thin pipe to create a solution increment.

Crush Ratio = [Thin Pipe] ÷ [What Goes In]

More precisely, the crush ratio for a given time period is the number of rocks out through the thin pipe in a given period of time divided by the number of rocks that come into the Rock Crusher during that same period of time.

At first glance, you might think that an ideal crush ratio is 1—whatever goes into the Rock Crusher results in valuable solution increments. Conventional thinking would see this as an indication that we are making efficient use of people's time, and would see any ratio significantly less than 1 as an indication that people's efforts are being wasted.

Reality is quite different. Such a high crush ratio suggests that the Rock Crusher is nothing more than a requirements queue and that these requirements are likely massively overprocessed—a significant Lean waste. A high crush ratio may also indicate that the development organization is overly cautious and very low on innovation. An innovative organization will typically pursue many options and be able to quickly eliminate options that have little hope of creating superior value.

At the other end, a crush ratio close to 0 indicates congestive collapse. Everyone is busy, but nothing is getting done. The organization is either incapable of completing things, or reluctant to pursue ideas to the end. Perhaps the organization is stuck chasing shiny things or the backlog owner cannot make timely decisions and the Rock Crusher workflow is drifting. A ratio of 0 may also result from serious conflicts between the different Rock Crusher ownership roles and, therefore, reflect constantly changing priorities.

An appropriate crush ratio for a value stream depends on the business context and where the solution is in its lifecycle. This is partly why most consultants prefix every answer with "it depends." After all, if it did not depend, then everything could be strictly rule-based and experience would not count for much.

One way to determine the appropriate crush ratio for a backlog is to consider it in terms of investment horizons—how much money and innovation the product requires. Borrowing from the Baghai investment model,[1] we describe three investment horizons which we can use as a guide for determining appropriate crush ratios.

Figure 13.1: The three investment horizons from *The Alchemy of Growth*

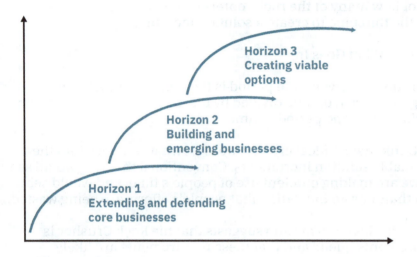

- Horizon 1 – Cash cow solutions, currently generating significant revenue.

- Horizon 2 – Emerging/growth solutions, starting to generate revenue. Some of these will be cash cows in a year or two; others will prove not viable and be retired.

- Horizon 3 – Incubating solutions, consuming cash. These are still in the research and development phase. Some solutions may become cash cows in three to five years; most will be shelved or canceled.

A very high crush ratio—say 80%—may be reasonable for a horizon 1 solution. The market needs at this horizon are very well understood, and the solution probably enjoys good brand recognition, so innovation is not as important. A very low crush ratio—say 20%—likely indicates considerable effort wasted on a stable product. For horizon 3, incubating solutions, a crush ratio of 80% would suggest that the organization is far too conservative and is not innovating, possibly risking its future viability.

1. Baghai, M., Coley, S., and White, D. *The Alchemy of Growth: Practical Insights for Building the Enduring Enterprise*. Basic Books. 2000.

Is It Working? Rock Crusher Metrics

The following table shows what we would consider acceptable crush ratio ranges in each of the Baghai horizons. Note that these are examples, not prescriptions; "it depends," and your situation may call for a different ratio.

Baghai Horizon	Crush Ratio	
Horizon 1 (Current)	80%–50%	This horizon represents real solutions currently in use by customers. The problem and solution are clear, and experimentation is much less frequent.
Horizon 2 (Emerging)	50%–25%	Refinement of emerging ideas requires substantial innovation but not as much radical experimentation as in Horizon 3.
Horizon 3 (Incubating)	25%–10%	Innovation and experimentation are rife in this horizon. Not every idea will be worth moving into Horizon 2, which is OK.

Like all metrics, the crush ratio is just an indicator and not an explanation. It is one more piece of data that may help us create a hypothesis of what is happening in the value stream. If, for example, the team discovers that flow loads are climbing, flow efficiency is dropping, and they have a very high crush ratio, it may suggest that they are unable to say no. If the crush ratio is very low in the same situation, the team could be spending a lot of time evaluating alternatives and new ideas that get discarded, without getting much done.

Hygiene Metrics

Hygiene metrics (sometimes called maturity or competency metrics) measure how well the team follows good Rock Crusher practices. Hygiene metrics are reasonable predictors of performance because the poor performance can often be traced back to poor hygiene. Hygiene metrics are much like the engine instrumentation in your car, such as water temperature and oil pressure. They cannot tell you much about where you are going, or how fast you are going, but they can tell you if your engine can get you there.

Hygiene metrics are usually captured in surveys, typically using a list of questions that a team answers using a 5-point scale. This survey shows one way of measuring good Rock Crusher hygiene.

	Strongly Disagree	Disagree	Neutral	Agree	Strongly Agree
Rocks are aged—we know when each rock came into the Rock Crusher and how long it has been there.	O	O	O	O	O
We regularly remove zombie rocks through the waste gate.	O	O	O	O	O
Rocks are clearly expressed, have an intent, and result in a verifiable model, which is tested and demonstrated.	O	O	O	O	O
We hold our backlog refinement meeting on a regular cadence.	O	O	O	O	O
Work intake is well defined, and all work requests pass through the backlog owner.	O	O	O	O	O

Hygiene metrics can indicate likely product quality issues. The healthier the team's hygiene metrics, the more likely they are to be effective at working together. An unhealthy team will probably struggle to jell as a team, is likely to default to work hand-offs rather than collaboration, and may be subject to internal politics and other inefficiencies.

There is no perfect set of metrics that can be applied to every organization. The Rock Crusher is a flow-based model, so metrics that provide insight into turbulence and flow rate can help in understanding the health of the value stream. But to gain useful insights, we must use the appropriate metrics, and must use those metrics appropriately. Avoid confusing outcome, performance, and hygiene metrics, and focus most of your effort and attention on outcome metrics that indicate real value delivered for the business.

Summary

- Appropriately used metrics are a powerful tool for learning how well the value stream performs.
- Metrics fall into three broad categories—outcome, performance, and hygiene.
- OKRs are a way to support alignment from business outcomes to delivery of individual rocks.
- The Rock Crusher is a flow-based model, so flow metrics can provide insights into the health of the value stream.
- The crush ratio is a Rock Crusher metric that helps the team understand the variability and turbulence in the flow of work through the value stream.

Try This

- Identify the metrics currently used in your value streams and categorize them as outcome, performance, or hygiene metrics.

- Identify any missing outcome metrics which could help make the flow of value visible.

- Calculate your current crush ratio across Baghai's three investment horizons. Is your crush ratio appropriate for each horizon? If not, how could it be improved?

14 The Rock Crusher at Scale

Learning Objectives

- Explain why scaling should not always be the automatic approach to coping with larger systems.
- List strategies for relieving the backlog owner's work load and describe the limitations of these strategies.
- List the five Rock Crusher scaling practices and describe how to use them to scale the Rock Crusher beyond a single backlog owner.

We have been deliberately vague about how big a Rock Crusher team is. Without stating a specific team size, we have implied that the team is small enough to effectively work with a single backlog owner. They have a regular team backlog refinement meeting and perhaps also a strategic refinement meeting. The team may also perform multi-horizon planning that includes both short-term horizon (iteration) planning and long-term horizon (release) planning.

This combination of practices may work effectively for a single team up to about 15 to 20 people; larger teams may need more formal ways of combining these practices. Most agile scaling frameworks—SAFe®, LeSS, Scrum@Scale, Nexus™ and others—provide guidance for using these practices with teams of teams and by delegating accountability and responsibility.

The key to successful scaling is maintaining alignment in a large team or team of teams and reducing coordination friction. We have identified five scaling practices for going big with the Rock Crusher and maintaining alignment with backlog management.

- **Do Not Scale**. Always ask why you are scaling and whether it's truly necessary.
- **Enlist the Village**. Offload backlog management responsibilities by explicitly delegating to members of the village.
- **Delegate Backlog Ownership Accountability**. Distribute backlog management accountability by delegating it to other local backlog owners.
- **Strategic/Tactical Refinement Meeting Split**. Use a strategic/tactical refinement meeting split as a coordination and alignment mechanism.
- **Multi-Horizon Planning**. Use multi-horizon planning to build a rolling wave of roadmap and maintain alignment between teams.

Scaling Practice 0: First, Do You REALLY Need to Scale?

Does delivering the solution truly require a large group of people to work closely together, or is someone empire-building? (A lot of people enjoy prefixing their role with "chief.") Scaling comes with increased coordination overhead. For example, SAFe is an excellent framework for getting 50-plus people to work together to deliver a solution. One of the authors successfully used SAFe on an initiative involving more than 2,000 people. However, SAFe adds a significant set of additional roles, practices, and ceremonies that could be unnecessary if delivering the solution really does not require 50 or more people to work closely together.

If you believe that throwing more people at a solution will enable you to deliver faster, then remember that time does not compress well. A staff year is not 730 people trying to get a job done before lunchtime (a running joke for many years at IBM). Coordination delays will rapidly negate the potential additional productivity of adding more individuals. These concepts have been well understood in software engineering since Fred Brooks wrote about them as early as 1974, and the underlying principle of Brooks' Law has not changed: Adding people to a late project will only make it later.[1]

Craig Larman, co-creator of LeSS, cautions that agile values and Scrum concepts all too often get lost as teams scale because the organization is so inflexible at scale. One of his examples is a candid retrospective of the original large-scale software development project, SAGE (Semi-Automatic Ground Environment), which was created in the 1950s and involved hundreds of people. One of the program directors commented that if he had to do it again, he would "find the 10 best people and write it themselves."[2]

The adoption of scaling frameworks is often proposed as a solution to an organizational and architectural problem in the team. Teams are often poorly organized by function (analysis, coding, testing), which results in tightly coupled dependencies and interteam hand-offs that must be coordinated to deliver a solution. Far too often, organizations attempt to solve this team coordination issue by organizing the functional teams as agile teams and adopting a scaling framework. A better solution would be to reorganize the teams as loosely coupled cross-functional teams that can independently deliver solution increments. Frameworks such as LeSS and Scrum@Scale strongly advocate for this strategy. For example, a stream-aligned team is a fully cross-functional feature team that can deliver end-to-end customer value sprint after sprint after sprint.[3]

1. Brooks, F. *The Mythical Man-Month: Essays on Software Engineering*. University of North Carolina. 1974.

2. Horowitz, E., ed. *Practical Strategies for Developing Large Software Systems*. Addison-Wesley. 1975.

3. Skelton, M., and Pais, M. *Team Topologies: Organizing Business and Technology Teams for Fast Flow*. IT Revolution. 2019.

The Rock Crusher at Scale

A feature team is an agile ideal because each feature team can independently deliver an end-to end or full-stack solution increment. This maximizes speed and minimizes coordination costs since the team has few, if any, interteam dependencies. This is an ideal structure if the solution's technical architecture can support such an approach and expertise is reasonably well distributed across the teams.

Another common reason for adopting scaling frameworks is to cope with the coordination problems caused by brittle, tightly coupled architecture. Conway's law suggests that a system's architecture will follow the communications path between teams.[1] If the architecture is brittle and tightly coupled, then team organization probably is, too. Before introducing a powerful scaling framework, it may be better to take a step back and review both the architecture of the system itself and makeup and interactions of the teams.

Therefore, the zeroth rule of scaling asks, "Why do we need to scale, and do we gain real economic benefit from scaling?"

Scaling Practice 1: Enlist the Village

The first step in scaling is to explicitly delegate village roles to team members. You should not just hope someone can take on the analysis of a feature; one or more team members should know that they are responsible for getting the analysis done.

As we've previously argued, the classical role of the product owner is close to impossible in most contexts. Even when the backlog owner responsibilities are distributed among the village members as described in chapter 3, the backlog owner must have good domain knowledge (to understand the value of the rocks) and must be readily available to team members (to explain the intention and value of the rocks). Scaling only increases the pressure on the backlog owner, making it necessary to delegate more responsibilities to village members.

When working with 10 to 20 people organized as two or three teams, the simplest approach is to hold a joint planning meeting attended by all members of all teams. We call this the "village mob." The village mob can plan together and then work relatively independently in their teams. Enlisting the village mob gives the backlog owner the resources needed to work with effectively across the individual teams. This style of planning also reduces individual demands on the backlog owner because involving everyone in the planning mob increases alignment.

---

1. Conway, M. *How Do Committees Invent? Datamation.* April 1968. https://www.melconway.com/Home/Committees_Paper.html.

This approach may be manageable for two or at most three feature teams with up to 20 people working closely together on a single solution. Such a large planning meeting may be viable for mature teams with an in-depth understanding of the product, technology, and process, but beyond this it will bog down quickly. Imagine conducting estimating poker with 20 or more people, especially a team without an in-depth understanding of the solution.

Things get ugly in all walks of life when a mob gets too large. When the village grows too large, it may be better to hold separate iteration planning meetings, with the backlog owner attending each one. When working with multiple teams, we strongly recommend that the teams all hold their planning meetings on the same day. With two teams, this is straightforward for the backlog owner: They can have one planning meeting in the morning and another in the afternoon. (If the iteration planning meeting takes more than a half day, this is a major indicator that your backlog refinement process is not working.) The logistics become challenging for three teams, because the backlog owner needs to attend three separate planning, refinement, review, retro, and stand-up meetings, possibly across multiple time zones.

Enlisting the village becomes critically important in this model because coordinating backlog owner availability for two or three teams may impede progress and decision-making. During backlog refinement meetings, the analysts and SMEs (subject matter experts) can step up to help the team refine the backlog. In this model, the analyst and SME can recommend rock priority and whether to keep or eject a rock, but cannot make this decision without the backlog owner.

Scaling Practice 2: Delegated Backlog Ownership Accountability

Beyond two or three teams, the village mob is not a powerful enough mechanism for managing the backlog. At this point, consider distributing backlog ownership accountability between a chief backlog owner who has overall accountability for the backlog and additional local backlog owners who are accountable for some portion of the local backlog.

Thoughts from Steve

One metaphor I like for this model is the structure of feudal societies, where the monarch held supreme authority but delegated local law-making to the vassal lords—as long as they enforced the monarch's will. For fans of *Dune* or of Klingon society, think of the relationship between the emperors and the great houses.

Methodologies like LeSS Huge, Scrum@Scale and SAFe explicitly call out this hierarchical relationship between product owners. LeSS Huge has a single product owner supported by multiple area product owners. Scrum@Scale has a product owner team with a chief product owner (CPO) who owns the backlog and collaborates with the individual team product owners. All the teams in Scrum@Scale pull their work from a single integrated backlog.

SAFe has a product management role analogous to the Scrum@Scale CPO and LeSS Huge Product Owner. The product manager owns a program backlog, and team product owners each own one of the decentralized team backlogs. (SAFe defers on how many product managers there can be, but usually one person fills this role.) The SAFe backlog structure differs significantly from Scrum@Scale because SAFe explicitly creates a hierarchical relationship between the product manager and product owner and a corresponding hierarchy between the program backlog of features and a team backlog of stories.

Figure 14.1: Distributed backlog ownership in different framework

Chief Backlog Owner

Chief Backlog Owner

SAFe Backlog Ownership Delegation

Scrum @ Scale Backlog Ownership Delegation

Team or Tactical Backlog Owner

Team or Tactical Backlog Owner

Team or Tactical Backlog Owner

Team or Tactical Backlog Owner

Team or Tactical Backlog Owner

Team or Tactical Backlog Owner

Solution

This distribution of backlog ownership accountability is probably adequate for 50 to 125 people organized as 5 to 12 teams. However, there are situations where solution delivery requires organizing and coordinating even larger teams of 500, 1,000, 2,000 people or more. In these extreme situations, a Scrum of Scrums-type CPO may be working with and coordinating dozens or even hundreds of product owners.

This, of course, is unreasonable, so we manage the complexity of distributed backlog ownership by going fractal: All the local backlog owners are organized into backlog owner teams with a local chief backlog owner. Then we go up a level and organize the various chief backlog owners into a chief backlog owner team, with a designated chief-chief backlog owner.

We will raise one very important caution flag here: When you are contemplating multiple levels of backlog owner delegation, please reconsider the zeroth law of scaling. Very few solutions require hundreds or thousands of people to deliver. Is a single, tightly integrated backlog delegated across multiple levels of teams the appropriate way to organize and coordinate people? Each level of delegation introduces significant coordination overhead. Does it really take an extremely large and tightly coordinated team to get the job done, or are you trying to solve an architectural or organizational design problem by introducing a complex, heavyweight coordination mechanism?

Scaling Practice 3: Using the Strategic Refinement Meeting to Coordinate and Maintain Alignment

Scaling Practice 3 builds on Scaling Practice 2 (delegating backlog ownership) because we need to maintain alignment among all the backlog owners. The strategic refinement meeting is used to maintain alignment between the chief backlog owner and local backlog owners. All the local backlog owners are invited to the strategic refinement meetings, where they help refine the backlog and coordinate their value delivery. Then the individual team backlog owners can work with their teams at their tactical refinement meetings to refine and plan their strategies for preparing the rocks.

Figure 14.2: Using the strategic refinement meeting to coordinate alignment between backlog owners

Typically, each team and their backlog owner will meet at least once a week to refine their portion of the backlog. The backlog owners will then hold a strategic refinement meeting at least once every two weeks (half the tactical meeting cadence) to review the entire backlog and ensure that it remains aligned with enterprise strategy. In the hopefully rare case of multiple delegation levels, a higher-level strategic refinement meeting may be necessary, where the chief-chief backlog owner (the chief of chiefs) meets with the chief backlog owner of each backlog owner team.

Scaling Practice 4: Multi-Horizon Planning

Multi-horizon planning aims to plan and replan a roadmap (rolling wave planning). During the SAFe PI planning ceremony, teams develop a roadmap of iterations to demonstrate that their objective for the program increment is reasonably credible. Product managers then maintain a roadmap of PIs to forecast a possible future for realizing their vision. In other agile methodologies, a release typically represents a roadmap of sprints. There can also be a higher-level roadmap or forecasted releases. Going up another horizon level to strategic or portfolio planning, we can create a roadmap of PIs or releases. The fractal nature of multi-horizon planning is often demonstrated using the agile onion diagram.

Figure 14.3: The "Agile Onion" Multiple Levels of Planning

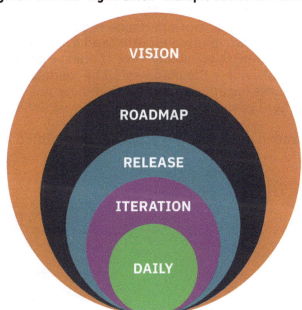

Multi-horizon planning is built into some methodologies. For example, SAFe PI planning is a marquee event. SAFe provides significant guidance for preparing and executing a PI planning event. In other methodologies, such as Scrum@Scale, multi-horizon planning is a suggested add-on with little guidance provided.

Exactly who participates in the various level planning meetings can differ. In SAFe, PI planning is an all-hands ceremony where everyone on the agile release train plans together with supporting stakeholders. But this type of "big room planning" predates SAFe and other formal scaling methodologies.

While there are huge benefits to big room planning, including alignment, dependency coordination, and resource balancing, the cost and logistics of this approach are significant and complex. Organizations not using SAFe may invite only key individuals to a release planning meeting—those who can speak authoritatively on the proposed work. This will likely include members of the village and select team representatives. This approach can work well for mature teams that are knowledgeable in their product domain and organized as feature teams with few dependencies. The risk is that the key individuals in the room may commit their teams to a schedule these teams do not support.

In all cases, the output of multi-horizon planning does not supersede regular team planning events. A PI or release typically spans two to three months, and a lot can happen during that period. The outcome of a release is usually a set of release goals, and any commitments made are to these goals, not to the plan itself. The roadmap of iterations created during this planning process only demonstrates that there is a credible and defensible path to reaching these goals.

Many organizations follow a three-level fractal model for this practice, exemplified by IIBA's multilevel planning horizon model.

Figure 14.4: IIBA's three-level multi-horizon planning model. (From _the Agile Extension to the BABOK_® _Guide_, v. 2. Courtesy of IIBA.)

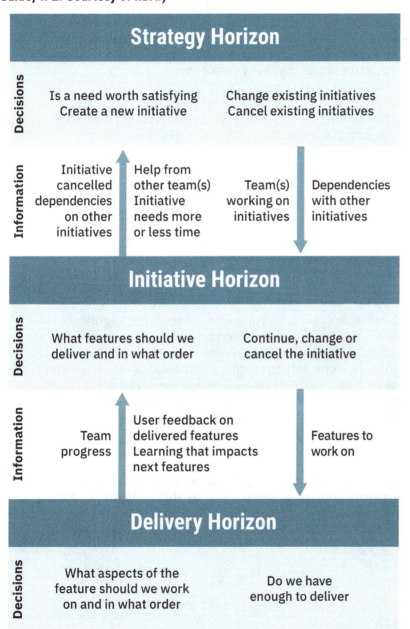

At the delivery horizon (the team level), teams follow their regular team planning practices. At the initiative horizon (the program level), teams perform big room planning or rely on delegates to plan a roadmap of iterations and PI or release goals. At the strategy horizon (the portfolio level), select individuals representing different products, programs, value streams, or business areas consider feedback from the lower planning levels, adjust the strategic plans, and integrate the revised milestones and desired outcomes into the initiative-level planning process.

Multilevel planning is based on trust, truth, transparency, and openness. All participants must feel safe challenging assumptions and reporting the actual truth about progress, impediments, and the learning that occurs at the lower levels. This is not a top-down cascade of directives; it is a collaborative conversation with information flowing in all directions, freely and safely.

Work Intake at Scale

A challenge when scaling backlog management is work intake. When and where are new rocks added to the backlog? Delegated backlog ownership, split refinement meetings, and multi-horizon planning all make the work intake process more complex.

A common anti-pattern is funneling new work requests through the highest-level planning horizon, which means the funnel is assessed at the strategic refinement meeting. The problem is that agile is about responsiveness, and it can be a long wait between strategic refinement meetings. For example, a portfolio-level refinement meeting may happen only once a quarter. This may be an acceptable delay for a large initiative, but if it takes a couple of months to decide on a simple work request, many stakeholders will find a back door to get their requests fulfilled. At its worst, this anti-pattern will return the team to the backlog as a reservoir model we are trying to get away from.

We recommend establishing a front-door intake process at every planning horizon. This means every team has a work intake—a funnel they evaluate during their refinement meeting. If there is an initiative or portfolio horizon, then there is an intake funnel the initiative or portfolio team evaluates at their refinement meeting.

A multilevel intake system requires intake policies for the various levels. Which rocks can the team evaluate at their tactical refinement meeting or even their daily stand-up? Which rocks should be sent to the strategy horizon and evaluated by the team at the strategic refinement meeting? If there is an initiative-level horizon, which rocks are appropriate at that level? Any enterprise using multi-horizon planning or splitting their refinement meetings needs to develop a multilevel intake policy. The following example shows a policy based on the forecasted rock size and cost risk:

- *Initiative Horizon.* Long-running rock greater than a quarter; for example, costs > $250K. Requires executive participation to vet.

- *Strategy Horizon.* Greater than a few weeks and less than a quarter; for example, costs $50K to $250K. Requires senior individuals (e.g., chief backlog owner or solution owner) to vet.

- *Delivery Horizon.* Less than a couple of weeks; for example, costs < $50K. Only requires the participation of the team and backlog owner.

The following table summarizes how the Rock Crusher scaling practices are applied in three of the scaling frameworks commonly in use today.

Comparison of Frameworks and Methodology Approaches for Backlog Scaling

Scaling Practice	SAFe	Scrum@Scale	LeSS
1. Enlist the Village	Offers some guidance for how a SAFe product owner collaborates with village-type roles such as business owners, epic owners, and customers.	No explicit guidance for specific roles beyond an emphasis on collaboration.	Calls out the five relationships a product owner needs to understand to work effectively with LeSS.
2. Delegate Backlog Ownership Accountability	Explicit hierarchical relationship between solution management, product management, and product owner. Team product owners are accountable for their team backlog.	Explicit hierarchical relationship between the CPO and team product owners.	Implicit relationship between the product owner for up to eight teams and a team representative. LeSS Huge has an area product owner as a designated role for more than eight teams.

Scaling Practice	SAFe	Scrum@Scale	LeSS
3. Strategic/ Tactical Refinement Meeting	Portfolio strategic review, solution sync, PO sync, and team backlog refinement.	Executive Action Team (EAT) scrum, backlog refinement.	Overall product backlog refinement.
4. Multi-horizon Planning	Explicitly implements multi-horizon planning with iteration and PI timeboxes.	Suggests use of release planning.	No explicit guidance.

Summary

- Before scaling your Rock Crusher, consider the zeroth rule: Do you truly need to scale? Are you trying to solve a coordination or architecture problem that's better addressed through other means?
- There are four main scaling practices. From least to most structure, these are: (1) enlist the village, (2) delegate backlog ownership, (3) implement strategic/tactical refinement structures, and (4) multi-horizon planning.
  - Scaling Practice 1 enlists the village by explicitly delegating village roles (e.g., analysis of a specific feature) to team members, to ensure work is allocated and people are accountable.
  - Scaling Practice 2, delegated backlog ownership accountability, offloads some of the backlog owner's logistics burden when working with two or three teams, and ensures faster decision-making and accessibility for low-level or urgent items. The strategic/tactical refinement split is often useful when adopting this practice.
  - Scaling Practice 3 leverages the strategic/tactical refinement meeting split to explicitly maintain alignment between the chief backlog owner and local backlog owners. It is mandatory if the team has adopted Scaling Practice 2.
  - Scaling Practice 4 uses multi-horizon planning to keep all teams aligned to a roadmap.
- Multi-horizon planning and multilevel backlog management require front-door intake processes for all levels of the process, to minimize backdoor requests from stakeholders who cannot wait the weeks or months between higher-level refinement meetings.

Try This

- What is driving you to consider scaling the Rock Crusher? Does the product or service you are developing really require you to "go big" with tightly coordinated teams of teams? Is someone empire-building? Are you using scaling practices to compensate for a brittle architecture?
- Roughly how many people need to work together to deliver a solution? How could you apply the Rock Crusher scaling principles to create the simplest solution that may work? What hypothesis could you create to test whether your approach is working?
- If you go big, what is an appropriate intake policy?

15 Implementing Your Rock Crusher

Learning Objectives

- List the eight steps in implementing a useful Rock Crusher.
- Explain why Rock Crusher implementation is a continuous process.

With any important business change, planning how you will implement the change is an important step. The Rock Crusher is no exception, and this chapter outlines one suggested approach to that process. We are not sitting next to you in your context, so take what we offer you here and adapt it to your situation. But be cautious about omitting or skipping components. Do not omit or massively change a step just because it's hard or painful. Implementation difficulties may imply a problem that you need to solve to improve flow.

There are eight steps in implementing the Rock Crusher as your backlog management model, each based on the answer to a question:

1. Form a Rock Crusher Hypothesis. (What problem are you trying to solve through adoption of the Rock Crusher approach?)
2. Choose a value stream. (Where will the Rock Crusher reside?)
3. Identify your village. (Who will play the various Rock Crusher roles?)
4. Visualize your Rock Crusher. (How will you visualize the rocks flowing through the Rock Crusher?)
5. Establish your intake policies. (Where are the front and back doors into the Rock Crusher?)

6. Establish your Waste Gate policy. (What are your policies for disposing of or managing the rocks ejected through the waste gate?)

7. Schedule the ceremonies. (What is the cadence and attendance list for the various Rock Crusher ceremonies?)

8. Continuously improve your Rock Crusher. (How will you apply continuous improvement concepts to the Rock Crusher you are implementing?)

We will examine each of these now.

Form a Rock Crusher Hypothesis

As part of good analysis practice, before doing anything you should ask questions:

- Why?

- What is the value of doing this?

- What problem are we solving?

- Why do we think this is the solution to this problem?

Just as agile business analysis starts with a hypothesis, you should start your Rock Crusher implementation with what could be called your Rock Crusher hypothesis. Borrowing from our model of well-formed rocks, this hypothesis will include a testable verifiable model—although your tests may be continuous and evolving (see Chapter 13 Is It Working? Rock Crusher Metrics).

To help you in writing your own hypothesis, here are a few starter statements:

- Implementing the Rock Crusher will improve our focus on valuable outcomes.

- Implementing the Rock Crusher will reduce the organizational load and waste by focusing work where it is expected to be valuable and eliminating work that would have been discarded anyway.

- Implementing the Rock Crusher will result in aligned organizational objectives, so that we spend more of our development effort on the higher-priority items and/or we complete more high-priority items because interfering requests have been eliminated.

- Implementing the Rock Crusher front-door and backdoor processes will improve use of team capacity, allowing us to react rapidly to emergencies and opportunities while still meeting strategic goals.

Creating a hypothesis is the start of a continuous improvement process. You will create Rock Crusher metrics that allow you to support or reject the hypothesis. This makes your testable verifiable model a source of knowledge that can drive process improvement. It also allows you to show how well your solution (the Rock Crusher) is addressing your enterprise need. The purpose of this exercise, after all, is to produce good outcomes for the enterprise. None of us will come to your workplace and give you a gold star because you created a textbook Rock Crusher. We will congratulate you for using the Rock Crusher model to understand and improve your workflow, and would encourage you to write a case study about it. We would also encourage case studies if the model fails in your environment, because there is often more learning in failure than in success.

Let us assume you took one of the example hypotheses from above: "Implementing the Rock Crusher will result in aligned organizational objectives, so that we spend more of our development effort on the higher-priority items and/or we complete more high-priority items because interfering requests have been eliminated." Here are some metrics you might consider:

- Total number of rocks accepted through the funnel

- Number of rocks that are identified as strategic

- Planned capacity allocated to strategic versus nonstrategic rocks

- Ratio of strategic versus nonstrategic rocks pulled through the thin pipe

- Effort spent on strategic versus nonstrategic rocks versus planned

Choose a Value Stream

The Rock Crusher is a flow-based model of backlog management, so to build a successful Rock Crusher you must understand how value flows in your organization. This understanding starts with some deceptively simple questions:

- What do you do that creates value?

- What is the solution you offer to your customer?

- How do you as an enterprise create and deliver that solution?

Your Product/Solution

It should be simple to say what valuable product or service you deliver to your customer, but many people are challenged to answer this question. It can instigate an existential crisis in organizations where everyone has a slightly different answer. Just ask people in your engineering and marketing groups and see if they give you the same answers. The question may be harder for organizations that offer a set of services rather than a tangible product.

Every organization, whether it is for-profit, nonprofit, humanitarian, or even governmental, exists to deliver something of value. Everyone has a product or service. Agilists most commonly work with for-profit companies providing goods or services that someone will pay for. But all the other cases also have some kind of product, whether it is acknowledged as such or not. Even an independent contractor such as an agile coach has a product. Their client is not paying for a coach's hours, but for the increased performance and agility that the client receives via the coach applying their knowledge and skill.

How Things Get Done

It is surprising how many professionals who can describe their valuable product are challenged to explain how they produce that value. Driving to this shared clear understanding within a group can be enlightening and valuable for any work team at any scale. It can also be difficult. We have been in value stream identification workshops where disagreements were so intense the facilitator had to call a pause.

Answering these two questions—what is valuable and how you create that value—gets to the heart of your value stream. A value stream is a powerful tool for visualizing and creating alignment around what is valuable and how things get done. Martin and Osterling highlighted the importance of understanding your value streams when they paraphrased Deming: "If you can't describe what you're doing as a value stream, you don't know what you're doing."[1] The process of understanding how value flows through the organization is called value stream identification.

Individuals and even whole departments often make the mistake of seeing the value flow only through the lens of their individual and siloed departments. This vertical perspective clouds the perception of the overall value stream and creates a flawed and fragmented view of the truth. This is how a value stream breaks, and often how the backlog becomes a buffering reservoir patching the break in the value stream.

1. Martin, K., and Osterling, M. *Value Stream Mapping: How to Visualize Work and Align Leadership for Organizational Transformation*. McGraw Hill. 2013.

Broken value streams are often the root cause of coordination delays and loss of customer focus.

Figure 15.1: We break the value stream and lose our customer focus when we view the value stream from a vertical perspective

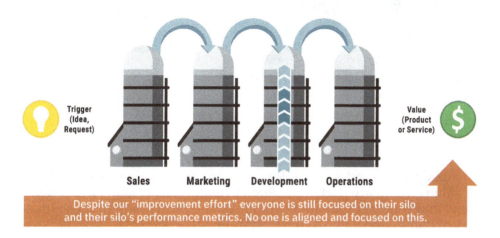

When trying to understand how value flows through your organization, take a "horizontal" perspective and envision how value flows from a customer point of view. Your company exists because of the value that customers receive, not because of the "value" an individual silo provides. You must understand how value flows across silos because the silos must collaborate to create the end value that the customer receives. Code may be a valuable asset, but there is no value created for the customer if it is not released, if it's not supported when it breaks, or if it doesn't do something the customer agrees is valuable in the first place.

Figure 15.2: When we view the value stream horizontally, from the customer's perspective, we get smooth unbroken flow

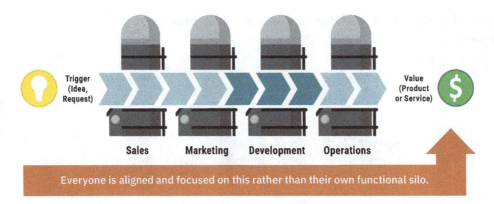

Once you have developed a clear and valid understanding of your value stream, identify which steps in that value stream are part of the Rock Crusher. Those steps will probably be value stream steps that represent the intake of ideas, the refinement of those ideas, and the end delivery of completed value to the customer.

Identify Your Village

Next you need to identify who will play each Rock Crusher role. In many organizations, the individual designated as the "product owner" is in reality what we would call a "solution owner." Determining the Rock Crusher ownership roles clarifies who is accountable and what they are accountable for. Determining roles also helps identify who is responsible and establishes the working relationships. It helps establish the go-to person for questions, and the attendee list for the refinement meetings.

The most important role to establish is that of the backlog owner. This is the person who is ultimately accountable for the backlog and has final say on prioritization. A common mistake is simply nominating a manager or subject matter expert for this role. While they may be knowledgeable, these people often do not have the time to be an effective backlog owner. More importantly, the organization at large has not invested them with the authority the backlog owner needs. Agile frameworks all require a point of content authority—a single point of content authority—for the backlog. This person must be able to say yes—and more importantly, no. Without this prerequisite, any agile framework will be hard pressed to succeed.

Thoughts from Ryland

I once worked with an agile coaching client who was going to turn their business analysts into product owners—backlog owners, in Rock Crusher terms—for their respective backlogs and teams. The leadership told me that the product owner would collaborate with various product managers to make sure that all the needs were met.

I challenged the leadership team with this: "That's fine, and collaboration is normal. However, the product owner's job is to own the backlog. They have that authority, and they will make decisions about how the team spends its capacity. There is almost never enough capacity to do everything that everyone wants, and someone has to make the important call here about that spend. You are making the BA that person.

"When you do that, the BA owns this responsibility to choose, and this is their authority and not the product managers'. Escalations can happen, but if everything is getting escalated you just are setting up a broken process. In other words, if you are OK with that

BA—who is now the PO—telling one product manager that the backlog will have their work in it and another product manager that there isn't room due to priority ... and if you expect those product managers to live with the answer, then I'm OK with the BA being the PO. So, are you OK with that?"

The leadership group paused, and then someone said, "Let us get back to you on that."

About three days later they got back to me and said "Yes, we are OK with it. We understand the implications and we'll have to see how it goes."

It turned out fine in this case. I'm glad I forced that issue early or it could have gone badly when the real decisions had to be made.

After you have identified the backlog owner you must identify what support they will need. Do you need additional people to serve as analysts? Is the backlog owner also the solution owner? Does the backlog owner need to coordinate with multiple solution owners? Who are the go-to subject matter experts able to answer detailed and specific questions about their topic? Is the backlog owner also a subject matter expert, or are there other subject matter experts you need to go to with occasional questions?

Visualize Your Rock Crusher

The four suggested Rock Crusher horizons—wishful thinking, speculative, forecasted, and ready—are just that, suggestions. The wishful thinking and speculative horizons are typically more turbulent, making it harder to force rank rocks. In the forecasted and ready horizons, the flow has stabilized more and it is possible and meaningful to force rank rocks. We suggested these horizons based on the patterns of turbulence we have observed at various clients and the degree of turbulence typically expected in the flow, but yours may vary. How turbulent is your flow, and how many horizons would you need to throttle and stabilize your flow?

Teams that have highly transactional work, are sufficiently tight knit, or have smaller overall initiatives may have a simpler Rock Crusher that just partitions the rocks that cannot be properly prioritized (force ranked) from the rocks that can. Other organizations may need more horizons to reflect their stabilization and throttling process. When designing your Rock Crusher, remember the words of Ron Jeffries: "Do the simplest thing that could possibly work."[1]

Getting Around Tool Limitations

A major challenge for the Rock Crusher is that most tools are workflow management and reporting systems and cannot manage turbulent flow. Tools have limited support for the exploratory dance of agile analysis. As a result, it is challenging if not impossible to visualize and manage the empirical nature of agile development. Most tools limit the parent-child hierarchy to two or maybe three generations and discourage ambiguity. For many tools, once a feature or story is created it is extremely difficult to split it, or even remove it. The tools almost lead us back to predictive planning.

To truly represent turbulent flow, a tool would need to not only permit but also support the following actions:

- Splitting a rock into multiple generations of parent-child relationships.
- Removing rocks that are no longer relevant and ejecting them through a waste gate. While this is not necessarily a tool restriction, many implementations restrict deletions because deleting rocks from their backlogs "messes up the reporting."

---

1. Jefferies, R. *Do the simplest thing that could possibly work.* 1998. https://ronjeffries.com/xprog/articles/practices/pracsimplest/.

- Visualizing the ambiguity in the ranking of rocks in earlier horizons rather than requiring forced ranking. We know of no backlog management systems which allow you to visually cluster a group of work items to reflect the uncertainty associated with the ranking of those items.

While most tools cannot directly implement a Rock Crusher model, there are many ways to approximate it, from a simple "cutline" to a sophisticated set of linked kanban boards. We offer three techniques here:

- Simple cutline—reasonable for a small, independent team

- Simple kanban board—applicable to a small to medium-sized team

- Linked kanban boards—appropriate for medium-sized to large teams and for team of teams

Depending on your tools and how "locked down" your environment is, you may have to rely on some supplemental tooling support to implement the Rock Crusher. If the tools are not completely locked down, some teams will create exploratory projects or workspaces that are not included in management reporting. Essentially, the supplementary projects and workspaces represent the Rock Crusher's funnel, and those used for reporting mostly represent the thin pipe.

Unfortunately, many tool environments are completely locked down. All workspaces use the same lifecycle model, and teams cannot even delete rocks from the backlog. This is often the case with cloud-based tools. This unfortunately leads to a lot of "off balance sheet" exploratory work that is not being visualized and managed. Some teams try to manage the exploratory work using spreadsheet tools such as Excel and wikis such as Confluence. Some teams have had good experiences using collaborative whiteboard tools such as Mural and Miro. These are reasonable work-arounds for agile tool limitations, but the risk of items falling through the cracks dramatically increases as you scale up the Rock Crusher.

Cutlines

For an individual or small team, possibly the simplest technique for approximating the Rock Crusher is a *cutline*. A cutline is simply a fake work item in the backlog that separates ready rocks from rocks that are not ready:

=============== **Ready** ==============

Rocks below this line are force ranked and ready. They meet the INVEST criteria.[1] Rocks above the cutline should not be assumed ready or force ranked. There is a high probability that rocks below the cutline will soon be pulled into an iteration. A good guideline is to have about one to two iterations worth of ready rocks; more than that likely represents overplanning or excess refinement.

Rocks above the cutline may not be sized beyond T-shirt sizing, or may not be sized at all. They may be large, perhaps classical epics too big to complete in an iteration. They may not yet have acceptance criteria and may still need additional learning to refine them. While the rocks may appear to be prioritized in the tool, they really are in loose clusters of priority.

Some teams may want to add a second cutline to separate forecasted rocks from speculative rocks:

=============== **Forecast** ===============

Rocks between "forecasted" and "ready" are being actively refined.

If there are more than two cutlines, a kanban board will be a better tool for representing the Rock Crusher.

Teams using the cutline method must diligently eject backlog items through the waste gate. This will keep the number of rocks manageable. Generally speaking, it is a best practice to keep fewer than 15 or 20 items in the backlog at any one time. (This will be part of your flow load metric, if you are using the flow framework.)

---

1. Wake, B. *INVEST in Good Stories, and SMART Tasks*. XP123 (blog). August 17, 2003. https://xp123.com/articles/invest-in-good-stories-and-smart-tasks/.

Implementing Your Rock Crusher

The advantage of this technique is its simplicity. For a small, tight-knit, fast-response development team, this may be more than adequate. The disadvantage of this technique is its limited ability to visualize the parent-child relationship between rocks. For a small team, this may not be a concern because the team can easily share knowledge informally. In a larger or more complex situation that may not be enough.

Simple Kanban Board

For a small team with a need for greater visibility, a simple kanban board will be an improvement. Most teams already have some kind of information radiator, usually in the form of a story board or kanban board that makes the state of their work visible. A team kanban board could look something like the figure below.

Figure 15.3: Typical team story board or kanban board

This type of team board generally only captures the flow from the backlog to done. Everything in the backlog, regardless of its readiness is simply in a "backlog" state.

The intent of the Rock Crusher is to make the steps required to get work ready visible so they can be effectively managed. A kanban board incorporating the Rock Crusher may look something like the figure below.

Figure 15.4: Simple kanban board implementing the Rock Crusher

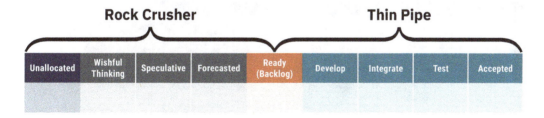

As with any good kanban board, there should be WIP (work in progress) limits on each step. Teams implementing Kanban best practices will have explicit exit criteria for each column (state) of the board. Ideally, those exit criteria express readiness in terms of how a rock passes some kind of test—either software or analysis.

Linked Kanban Boards

The Rock Crusher can be scaled by using the linked hierarchy approach. In this case, teams are collaborating to deliver a common solution and so share a common backlog. However, each team will have its own tactical kanban board for their development cycle. Much like the single team case, the strategic kanban board represents the lifecycle of big rocks and the multiple team kanban boards represent the lifecycle of smaller rocks that individual teams are executing or refining.

Figure 15.5: Multiple team kanbans

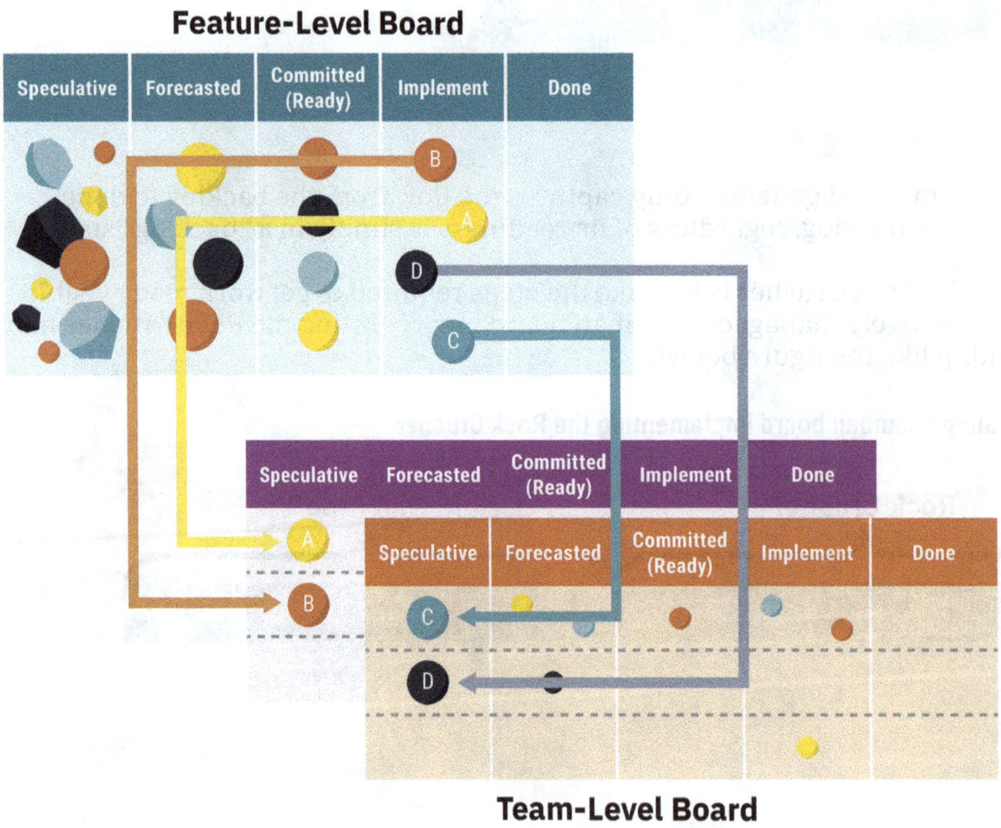

Implementing Your Rock Crusher

Establish Your Intake Policies

Intake policies establish how and when we will accept rocks. The formal or front-door intake policy sets down the rules for when the backlog owner and team will consider rocks that have arrived at the top of the funnel. For teams following capacity-based and timebox-based methodologies like Scrum or XP, this will be the usual planning and refinement meetings. For a team using a flow-based methodology like Kanban, the team will need to establish a schedule that maintains both flow and responsiveness.

Teams using Scrum or XP find their biggest challenge with handling "injections." Injections are rocks that arrive in the funnel during the execution of an iteration with an implied need to add the rock to the team's commitment for the current iteration. Injections should be considered unplanned non-roadmapped work as described in Chapter 9 Handling Rocks on and off the Roadmap.

Most environments will have to answer these questions:

- **Will you even consider injections?** Many teams take a hardline stance on this. The sprint commitment is held as a paramount concern by these teams. In Scrum this is called "sprint integrity," and in any sprint-based approach it is a very important concern. Routinely violating sprint integrity is an issue and is a bad or worst practice. We discuss ways of evaluating and handling this in Chapter 9 Handling Rocks on and off the Roadmap.

- **How responsive must you be to your stakeholders?** If the team needs to be more responsive to their stakeholders, then then they need some way to consider, accept, and reject injections. They must decide when they will meet to consider injections and who must be part of that conversation. Having a defined process for change and adaptation is important. Since you are accepting injections, the team should not be scrambling or disrupted when handling them.

- **If you accept the injection, then how will you change your commitment?** The team's capacity does not change just because an injection occurs. The capacity was probably fully allocated (to tolerance levels) at sprint planning. If your policy is to accept injections, then it is important that you respect their capacity limits by not overloading them and maintaining a sustainable pace. You need to make it clear that if the team accepts the injection you must also know whether it is displacing a committed rock, whether the team is accepting this as a new commitment, and possibly even the capacity cost of taking the rock in midsprint. For example, an injection related to the work the team routinely does may be a minor disruption. At the other extreme, something totally unusual and that requires new technologies may incur an evaluation cost for several senior team members just to define and size it on a rush basis.

As part of re-evaluating their commitment, the team should also track how much disruption and extra cost is incurred by injections. This will lead to an understanding of how this affects the overall flow and how much of this kind of disruption can be tolerated before the team declares an abnormal iteration.

Finally, you need to consider your backdoor policies—how you will handle direct stakeholder engagement with team members. Many teams will declare that all injections are referred to the backlog owner and therefore enter through the front door. A team needs to decide whether small backdoor efforts reduce friction in the organization and build goodwill or place the team's sprint commitment at risk.

Establish Your Waste Gate Policy

The waste gate is an important differentiator between the "stack of plates" model and the Rock Crusher. What goes in must come out. There is simply no way everything that goes into the Rock Crusher will get done, so some of the rocks absolutely must exit via the waste gate.

Your waste gate policies must be clear. This will eliminate the risk of zombie rocks clogging the Rock Crusher. It will also ensure that you do not prematurely bury rocks that may still have some value.

Here are some things to consider when deciding these policies:

- How much WIP is too much? Establishing WIP limits for important work stages is generally considered a best practice.

- What happens to rocks that are sent to the waste gate? This will happen at various times. Are these rocks deleted from the tool or moved to some kind of deferred or archived state?

- How will rocks be aged out? When is a rock too old to be retained? It is shocking how many teams will have stories in their backlog that are years old, with minimal likelihood they will ever be implemented. How long should a story-sized rock remain in the ready state? A quarter? A half year? A year? How about a feature-sized rock? How long should an initiative-sized rock remain in the speculative state?

When the team follows good practices for backlog hygiene, they won't have to waste as much time and effort managing noise and distractions in the backlog.

Schedule the Ceremonies

Teams following good agile practices will already have a standing backlog refinement meeting on their calendar. What may change with the adoption of the Rock Crusher model is who is invited to that meeting and whether the team adopts a strategic/tactical refinement meeting split.

Continuously Improve Your Rock Crusher

If you now have a viable Rock Crusher implementation, congratulations! You should be proud of this accomplishment. You now have an experiment to validate your Rock Crusher hypothesis. Like good scientists, and in alignment with our verifiable model and agile thinking, you will run the experiment, collect data, and review the data.

Your practices for embracing change will change as you learn. The world around you is constantly changing, which means the Rock Crusher experiment never ends.

Final Advice

Alistair Cockburn once described good software processes as "barely sufficient."[1] Start with your Rock Crusher hypothesis: Why are you doing this and what problem are you trying to solve? How will you know that you have solved it? For a tight-knit team of three or four people, the cutline method may work. For a slightly larger team, a single kanban board might do it. For a team with significant analysis and design work, linked kanban boards are probably a good starting point, and of course a large team of teams may have several hierarchies of linked kanban boards.

That said, the Rock Crusher has a few important traits which must not be omitted. Consider these hygiene statements part of the test applied to the verifiable model.

- Is there an identifiable value-creating solution? A value stream for creation of that solution? Is the value stream mapped to the Rock Crusher and the thin pipe?

- Is one person clearly identified as the owner of the backlog? Is at least one person clearly identified as the solution owner? Is there a clearly identified team that pulls rocks through the thin pipe?

- Are there clearly stated front-door and backdoor intake policies?

1. Cockburn, A. *Agile Software Development*. Addison-Wesley. 2001.

- Is there a waste gate and a clearly stated policy for ejecting rocks through the waste gate? What happens to rocks that are ejected?

- Can you visualize the Rock Crusher and thin pipe, whether it's with your tooling or just sticky notes on the wall?

- Do you clearly understand the definition of a well-formed rock in your context? Do you have a clear definition of ready?

- Do you consistently see well-formed rocks that include both a hypothesis and a testable verifiable model?

- Is there a regularly scheduled refinement meeting? If needed, are there additional horizon-centric meetings, aligned to the horizons which best suit your business needs?

- Do you have a suite of metrics aligned with your solution and your value stream? Do your metrics include the historic crush ratio as well as metrics identifiably aligned with outcome, process, and hygiene concepts?

- Are you continuously experimenting to improve your process and outcomes through retrospectives, wise use of metrics, and frequent collaboration and consultation with your team and your customers?

If you have solid positive answers to these questions, you're probably doing OK.

Methodologies for Inspiration

For a small team, building a Rock Crusher is reasonably straightforward. The "simplest thing that could possibly work" will be fairly easy to decide among themselves, and many cracks and gaps in implementation hygiene are easily corrected by team-shared tacit knowledge. If the small group takes an experimental and learning mindset toward the development of their Rock Crusher, this will naturally grow and evolve over time.

Designing a Rock Crusher from scratch for a larger team is much more challenging. Some of the scaling frameworks provide useful guidance to help you get started.

SAFe®. SAI's SAFe framework is an excellent guide for using the Rock Crusher at scale and illustrates multiple planning horizons and using linked kanban boards as backlog management (much like the Rock Crusher). The downside of SAFe is that it is intended for environments where at least 50 people must work tightly together to deliver a solution. SAFe is one well-used starting point for scaling frameworks, but it is not the end of any scaling journey. A team adopting SAFe to inform its way of working should be constantly learning and experimenting, mastering SAFe and then finally evolving it in a disciplined manner as the team evolves.

Implementing Your Rock Crusher

LeSS and Scrum@Scale. Like SAFe, LeSS and Scrum@Scale are frameworks for organizing many people to get a job done. Unlike SAFe, LeSS and Scrum@Scale try to remain strongly bound to the Scrum philosophy and practices. Both provide guidance for how multiple Scrum teams can coordinate and pull their work from a single backlog. One key differentiator between LeSS and Scrum@Scale is LeSS's emphasis on experimentation and learning. These are good frameworks for when you are able to organize your Scrum teams as feature teams and minimal coordination is required between teams.

Disciplined Agile®. Another useful source of guidance is PMI's Disciplined Agile (DA) which is a process construction framework. Following the mantra "choice is good," DA creates a set of process goals and offers alternatives for implementing those goals. One awesome DA feature is the goal graphs that it explains the trade-offs between the different implementation alternatives. DA is an excellent reference to help inform your choices for implementing a Rock Crusher.

The Spotify Model. We mention Spotify last and only to call out that it *cannot* provide guidance for creating a Rock Crusher. Henrik Kniberg's[1] white paper on the software engineering culture at Spotify inspired many people. Despite admonishments from Kniberg and others not to copy Spotify, some 5% of the industry claims they are using what is now called "the Spotify model" in their environment. While the Spotify model provides some guidance for the organization of teams and team of teams, it provides very little guidance on how to manage a backlog and therefore is not a good model for providing guidance on the Rock Crusher.

1. Kniberg, H. *Spotify Engineering Culture (part 1)*. crisp. 2014. https://blog.crisp.se/2014/03/27/henrikkniberg/spotify-engineering-culture-part-1.

Summary

- The Rock Crusher itself must have a hypothesis, a verifiable model, and an applied test.
- Metrics should be identified and used to guide Rock Crusher progress and show the value of the process.
- Recognize that it takes a village when forming your Rock Crusher process. The backlog owner, a key member of the village, must be explicitly identified by the organization and their authority must be recognized.
- Both front-door and backdoor intake processes should be identified, monitored, and used correctly.
- Value stream mapping is essential for success when implementing the Rock Crusher. The Rock Crusher will connect at important points to the value stream, but it is unlikely to connect at every point. The critical moments are work intake, refinement, the thin pipe, and the waste gate.
- Value streams must be considered across functional areas and must focus on the creation of end customer value. Intermediate steps are only important as part of the path and not as full value paths of their own.
- Cutlines, kanban boards, and linked kanban boards can all assist with management.
- Anyone implementing a solution should consider developing policies to guide Rock Crusher practices. This will help avoid clogging the system, eliminate waste, and maximize throughput as well as value.

Try This

- Dump your existing backlog of not-closed items into a spreadsheet. Include attributes such as item type (epic, feature, story), date created, last updated, and current status. Analyze the backlog to see how old the items are and locate possible zombie items in the backlog. What is the age distribution of the various items? Can you suggest rules the team could adopt for automatically using the waste gate on aged items?
- Consider the roles and responsibilities of the team members. Can you identify the backlog owner? Do they have the level of authority needed by that role? What other roles are present and who occupies those roles?
- What horizons might best fit the needs of your team and organization? Can you name and describe the time frames you might use? How many do you need?

Glossary

A Analyst Someone responsible for transforming the sometimes competing needs, wants, hopes, interests, and aspirations of the customers, stakeholders, and solution owner-as well as the contributions of subject matter experts-into a shared, clear understanding of precisely what to build-the solution.

B Back Door An expedited path for requirements, bypassing the backlog owner and a lot of organizational processing; for example, when a stakeholder directly approaches their favorite team member with a request. The back door represents the official rules for breaking the intake rules. See front door.

Backlog A list of the new features, changes to existing features, bug fixes, infrastructure changes, or other activities that a team may deliver in order to achieve a specific outcome. The backlog is the single authoritative source of things that a team works on. That means that nothing gets done that isn't on the product backlog. Conversely, the presence of a backlog item on a backlog does not guarantee that it will be delivered. It represents an option the team has for delivering a specific outcome rather than a commitment.[1]

1. The Agile Alliance. *Glossary: Product Backlog.* https://www.agilealliance.org/glossary/backlog.

	Backlog Item	See Rock.
	Backlog Owner	The person accountable for prioritizing all rocks in the backlog so that the team is doing the most valuable work.
C	Crush Ratio	A measure of how much work entering the Rock Crusher is ultimately pulled through the thin pipe to create a solution increment-the ratio of overburden to valuable ore.

Crush Ratio = ThinPipe / WhatGoesIn

	Crusher	A special rock added to the backlog during a refinement meeting to acquire the knowledge required to refine rocks. Crushers make the refinement process visible, and therefore manageable.
	Customer	The receiver or beneficiary of the solution. They may need to be informed about decisions affecting the solution.
I	Intent	The outcome the team seeks from completing a rock and successfully testing its verifiable model.
F	Flow	The movement of knowledge and materials through a value stream.
	Forecasted	A textbook Rock Crusher readiness horizon where flow is significantly smoothed. Forecasted rocks are near ready, with a good degree of certainty that the team will commit to them, and are nearly or completely force ranked.
	Front Door	The official rules for intake, which directly involve the backlog owner in the decision-making process. See Back Door.

	Funnel	The turbulent flow of rocks is throttled and stabilized in the funnel. The Rock Crusher funnel shifts our mental model of the backlog from a passive reservoir to an active learning and discovery process that results in a stabilized and throttled flow.
R	Ready	A textbook Rock Crusher readiness horizon where flow is smooth and rocks are force ranked.
	Readiness Horizons	Boundaries reflecting the relative turbulence in the flow and readiness of rocks within the horizon. The textbook Rock Crusher has four suggested readiness horizons: wishful thinking, speculative, forecasted, and ready.
	Rock	A backlog item; a description of a specific outcome or piece of work in a team's backlog. Backlog items may be formatted as user stories, technical stories, defect fixes, refactorings, crushers, and so on. All rocks must have an intent, a verifiable model, and a test.
S	Solution	The product or service offered to the customer. A solution may be a product for sale, a contracted deliverable, or an organizational asset used to support or build the products and services an organization offers.
	Solution Increment	A small, demonstrable piece of the solution that can be integrated into the solution.
	Solution Owner	The person accountable for delivering the solution.
	Speculative	A textbook Rock Crusher readiness horizon where the flow is less turbulent than wishful thinking, but with only a moderate degree of certainty that all or part of the intent described by the rock will be needed or done (e.g., moderate to large epic user stories).

Splitting	Breaking up a large, reasonably well-defined rock into two or more smaller rocks at roughly at the same level of abstraction as the original rock in order to right-size it for implementation.
Stakeholder	Any individual who, at a minimum, must be consulted about precisely what is being built, and who may also have decision-making authority about what is built.
Strategic Refinement Meeting	A backlog refinement meeting that focuses on determining whether the rocks align with strategic organizational objectives.
Subject Matter Expert (SME)	Someone with in-depth knowledge of a relevant problem domain and/or relevant solution technology and development practices. SMEs use their knowledge to advise other roles in deciding precisely what to build. They are responsible for providing the expertise other roles may need to perform their jobs.

T

Tactical Refinement	A backlog refinement meeting that focuses on the execution needs of getting rocks ready to pull through the thin pipe. Rocks brought to the tactical refinement meeting are usually in the forecasted or ready horizons.
Team	A close-knit group of individuals who collaborate to pull work through the Rock Crusher and thin pipe to deliver solution increments. Our use of the team is generic and can represent anything from a small classic Scrum team of 7+/-2 to a large team of teams.
Thin Pipe	The solution development steps that pull ready rocks from the Rock Crusher to deliver solution increments.

V Verified Model

The work product of any rock which may be subjected to testing. The tests are asserted as part of the rock, often in the form of acceptance criteria. Upon delivery of the rock, passing the test(s) proves that the rock satisfies its intent and the rock is accepted by the backlog owner. The Rock Crusher has three levels of verification based on objectivity. See Intent.

Village

A metaphor highlighting all the roles required to operate The Rock Crusher and take an idea from concept to cash. The village represents roles and not specific individuals.oncept to cash using The Rock Crusher.

W Waste Gate

An explicit process for ejecting rocks from the Rock Crusher that will not be completed. Rocks may be ejected through the waste gate actively (because the rock is not valuable) or passively (because they have aged out).

Wishful Thinking

A textbook Rock Crusher readiness horizon reflecting a highly turbulent flow where the ideas likely change frequently and are only moderately defined. Rocks in this horizon may not even pass vetting.

Index

V

W

Index

About the Authors

Steve Adolph

Steve started his career in engineering and building telephone switches and railway signalling systems. Around the late 1990's he moved into management where he became interested in the outsized influence ways of working and organizational culture have on enterprise outcomes. Steve became interested in agile when he started collaborating with Pattern Language aficionados at the PLoP conferences. Today, he works as an agile coach with cprime (Canada).

Steve has a PhD in electrical and computer engineering. Steve has numerous publication credits including the book *Patterns for Effective Use Cases* and was a member of the core team that developed IIBA's *The Agile Extension to the BABOK® Guide* version 2.

Shane Hastie

Shane has been a practitioner and leader of developers, testers, trainers, project managers, and business analysts, helping teams to deliver results that align with overall business objectives for over 35 years.

Shane was a director of the Agile Alliance from 2011 to 2016 and was the founding Chair of Agile Alliance New Zealand. He leads the Culture and Methods editorial team for InfoQ.com where he hosts the weekly InfoQ Culture Podcast. He is also co-chair of the Agile Alliance Agile Coaching Ethics initiative, working to produce a code of ethical conduct for agile coaching. He is an ICF registered Professional Coach.

He was one of the authors of *The Agile Extension to the BABOK® Guide* versions 1 and 2 and a member of the core team for *A Guide to the Business Analysis Body of Knowledge (BABOK® Guide)* version 3. He is coauthor of the recent book *#noprojects: A Culture of Continuous Value*.

Shane has a Master of Information Management from Victoria University of Wellington and is an ICAgile Certified Expert in both Product Ownership and Agile Coaching. He is CBAP #140.

Ryland Leyton

Ryland Leyton is a business analyst, author, speaker, educator, agile coach, and technology translator. He has worked in the technology sector since 1998, starting off with database and web programming, gradually moving through project management, and eventually finding his passion in growing the agile practices and analysis skills of individuals, teams, and companies.

Ryland is an active member of IIBA, and speaks often on topics including business analysis, project management, agility, and career development. His professional contributions include being a member of the core team for the *Agile Extension to the BABOK® Guide* version 2, as well as the IIBA Agile Analysis Certification.

Involvement in IIBA projects grew from Ryland's 2015 book T*he Agile Business Analyst: Moving from Waterfall to Agile*, which is considered a standard for business analysts working in agile situations. His 2019 book It's About Your Career: Skills for a Lifetime of Loving Your Work! grew from his drive to pass along lessons and gifts from important people in his professional life.

Ryland can be reached via www.RylandLeyton.com.